Robin

The Pocket Essential

THE RISE OF NEW LABOUR

www.pocketessentials.com

First published in Great Britain 2002 by Pocket Essentials, 18 Coleswood Road,
Harpenden, Herts, AL5 1EQ

Distributed in the USA by Trafalgar Square Publishing, PO Box 257, Howe Hill
Road, North Pomfret, Vermont 05053

A CIP catalogue record for this book is available from the British Library.

ISBN 1-903047-83-8

2 4 6 8 10 9 7 5 3 1

Book typeset by Pdunk
Printed and bound by Cox & Wyman

CONTENTS

Introduction

What This Isn't

This isn't a bite-sized summary of all the books written about New Labour and its personnel synthesised into a nice neat narrative for the busy reader. Some of those books *are* cited here and some are not. Most of those I have read are pretty poor, the best bits generally being accounts of who hates whom and why, who stabbed whom in the back or leaked what to which journalist. Some of this is entertaining but little of it is of any importance.[1]

Nor is this an account of the stage-by-stage takeover of the Labour Party's organisation by the tiny group who called themselves 'New Labour.'[2]

Nor is this an attempt to make sense of the term 'New Labour' or to provide a coherent account of its ideology. New Labour was simply copied from the American Democratic Party - there was a brief period when Bill Clinton tried and failed to get 'New Democrats' into general use - and is simply a piece of banal rebranding which means little. New Labour's ideology is a hodgepodge of opportunism, sound bites, kowtowing to powerful interests and attempts to copy America. The whole mess is validated or rejected by opinion sampling conducted by Philip Gould.

What This Is

This short book contains a brief account of what is best described as the American tendency in the Labour Party: from Hugh Gaitskell in the 1950s to the formation of the Social Democratic Party in the 1980s, and then into the rise of New Labour from the Labour election defeats of that decade. Another theme is the changes in Labour's economic policies central to and accompanying the rise of New Labour. Economics may sound dull but what I mean by economics is more like economic politics. In this case, the imposition of the ideology of the City of London on the rest of the economy by the Conservative Party led by Mrs Thatcher - and how Labour came to accept it. En route, there are accounts of some of the little-known aspects of the biographies of the New Labour faction's leading members and an account of how the faction's thinking, especially its obsession with imitating the United States, led to its present role as international boosters for globalisation and transnational capital.[3]

One of the most fatuous things Tony Blair tried to do before Labour won the election of 1997 was the brief attempt to rebrand Britain the previous year: 'Britain: A Young Country' and 'New Britain' were the catch-phrases.[4] Of course, this is a very old country. Blair's own party is over 100 years old and even the faction within it which he represents can be traced back to the beginnings of the Cold War half a century ago.

The rise of New Labour is the consequence of events in the 1970s and 80s. Labour was perceived - wrongly - to be economically incompetent and to be responsible for the inflation and the industrial trouble of the late 1970s. This lost them the 1979 election. Taking office promising to reduce unemployment, the Conservative Party, led by Mrs Thatcher, promptly tripled unemployment (from 1 million to 3 million) and would have been turned out of office in 1983 had it not been for the appearance, in time for the election, of the Social Democratic Party which took millions of votes off Labour. Mrs Thatcher won again (with a little boost from the Falklands War) and, with North Sea oil revenues to keep the ship afloat, set about the Tory 'counter-revolution.' They privatised the nationalised industries, sold council houses, smashed the trade unions and redistributed wealth from bottom to top.

Having lost again in 1987, under Neil Kinnock and then John Smith, Labour began to remodel itself on the apparent electoral popularity of Thatcherism (I say apparent because the Conservative Party never won even 50% of the votes between 1979 and 1992) and the apparently over-whelming power of the City of London, whose policies the Conservatives had been implementing.

In 1977 I went to a meeting in a pub in the Lake District at which the local Tory MP addressed an audience mostly consisting of hill farmers. The farmers believed that it was Labour Party policy to nationalise the land. The meeting was generous enough to let me, their urban visitor, speak but nothing I said made any difference to this belief. (Nothing I *could have said* would have made any difference.) That was the first time I can remember realising that in politics what people *believe* to have taken place can be more important than historical reality. Some of the people *are* fooled some of the time. Between 1979 and 1992 enough of the people were fooled into blaming Labour for the inflation created by Edward Heath to return four Conservative Governments. We are still living with the consequences of this.

Notes

Some of this book is ground I have covered before in my writing in *Lobster, Variant* and also in my 1997 book *Prawn Cocktail Party*. I am grateful to the publishers of the Pocket Essentials series for giving me the chance to have another tilt at this material because *Prawn Cocktail Party* was mangled by its publisher.

1. A good example is Julia Langdon's *Mo Mowlam: The Biography* (London: Little,Brown, 2000), which is full of fascinating bits of gossip (including comments that Gordon Brown doesn't get on with women; nudge, nudge) but when it comes to Mowlam's role, say, in the campaign with the late John Smith to persuade the City of London to accept the Labour Party, Langdon tells us almost nothing at all about Mowlam's views on this or what she did. Indeed, Langdon manages to write an entire book about Mowlam without really conveying what, if anything, Mowlam believed or wanted to do. The thought does occur that maybe Mowlam believed nothing much. On the other hand, the reader learns much about Mowlam's touchy-feely personality and her ability to shock and manipulate the orthodox middle classes by talking about her bowels, her periods etc. Not mentioned by Langdon, but found in Andrew Rawnsley's *Servants Of The People* (London: Penguin, 2001), was Mowlam's habit of holding conversations while on the toilet with the door open - something also practised by the late Robert Maxwell and Lyndon B Johnson. What this means...

2. The outline of this can be seen in the John Rentoul biography of Tony Blair, *Tony Blair* (London: Little,Brown, 1995) or in Philip Gould's account, *The Unfinished Revolution* (London: Little,Brown, 1998).

3. Tony Blair, *New Britain: My Vision Of A Young Country* (London: Fourth Estate, 1996). I confess I failed to read this mind-numbingly boring book. I have picked it up many times but failed to read any chapter in its entirety. Perhaps I am doing Mr Blair an injustice. The book may not have been published to be read but simply as a platform for the slogans 'New Britain' and 'Britain: A Young Country.' These were attempts to rebrand Labour so that they would be more acceptable to the focus groups being run by Philip Gould, groups that were central to the Blair/Brown faction's policy-making. The 'New Britain' and 'Young Country' nonsense appeared also in Peter Mandelson and Roger Liddle's *The Blair Revolution: Can Labour Deliver?* (London: Faber and Faber, 1996) of the same year. In *Alastair Campbell: New Labour And The Rise Of The Media*

Class (London: Aurum Press, 1999), Peter Oborne cites the Blair book as a key source on 'New Labour English,' that curious verb-free guff which its spokespersons have learned to speak. Oborne's book is the best one on New Labour to date.

4. *The Guardian* reported in 'Finance Notebook' on 16 June 2001 (the day after I wrote the sentence to which this note is attached) page 27, first paragraph, that on Wednesday of that week Rupert Murdoch had visited the Chancellor of the Exchequer, Gordon Brown, and that on Friday the inquiry by the Office of Fair Trading into the dominance of pay-for-view TV in the UK by the Murdoch-owned BSkyB had been delayed for three months. Is this Government, with a Commons majority of nearly 150 and the Opposition in tatters, still afraid of the Murdoch-owned media? Apparently so.

1. Myths And Delusions

The Blair faction rose to influence within the Labour Party as a consequence of the four election victories by the Conservative Party: Mrs Thatcher in 1979, 1983 and 1987; and John Major in 1992. This may seem so obvious as to be barely worth stating but it is important: New Labour and the policy changes it has wrought were the consequences of electoral defeat, not considered evaluation and reflection. Would we now be embarking on the part-privatisation of the NHS and the London Tube if Labour had won the 1987 or 1992 elections? I doubt it. That series of Conservative victories was based on the central political myth of our time in the UK: the myth of the Labour Party's economic incompetence. For almost twenty years a substantial chunk of the British electorate believed that Labour could not be trusted with the economy. The Conservatives won the 1979 election because enough of the electorate were persuaded that Labour had made a mess of the economy in the 1970s, causing hyperinflation. This led to the industrial trouble of 1978/9, the so-called 'Winter of Discontent,' with its images of uncollected rubbish, unburied bodies and the attendant notions of union bullies and anarchy.

In fact the inflation of the 1970s was almost entirely created by Edward Heath who led the Conservative Party to victory in the election of 1970. Heath had one overriding aim: British entry into the European Economic Community (EEC). Everything else played second fiddle to that.[1] In the first year and a half of his government he apparently believed that the best way to prepare the British economy for entry into the expanded EEC was a dose of competition and freedom, which are the traditional Tory Party ideas of getting the government off the backs of the producers, reducing taxation and so forth. Heath appeared to believe that, under these conditions, British capitalism would produce the investment and modernisation required to meet the impending bracing winds of competition from Europe. But Heath discovered that British capitalism was not as enthusiastic about this as he was.

> 'So British business had failed to respond to the new climate of enterprise which the government had striven to create after 1970. As a result, Heath now believed the government had no choice but to take an active hand itself. Two years as Prime Minister had quickly disillusioned him as to the energy and even the patriotism of British industrialists who, he felt, had let him down.'[2]

11

This persuaded Heath 'that the government had no choice but to intervene directly to promote rapid growth - whatever ministers might have said previously about government getting off industry's back.'[3] This was Heath's famous U-turn. To achieve this he created a secret Whitehall committee in 1971 to devise a framework for industrial expansion.[4] It contained members of the government's think-tank, the Cabinet Office, Sir Leo Pliatzky of the Treasury and Sir William Neild, previously the Permanent Secretary at the Department of Economic Affairs of the outgoing Wilson Government.[5] It was this group which produced the 1972 Industry Bill that gave the state such power over industry that Tony Benn welcomed it as doing 'the spade work of socialism.'[6] So secret was this committee's work that even the Chief Secretary to the Treasury, Patrick Jenkin, was unaware of the Industry Bill until it was announced in the House of Commons.[7] It was this committee which produced the prices and incomes policy which followed the Industry Bill and which was to dog the Heath administration for the rest of its term in office.[8]

Without informing his party, and with only a small majority in the House of Commons, Heath tried to covertly reconstruct the British economy along continental European lines. He wanted to remake British industrial relations to resemble those in Germany[9] and introduced his industrial relations legislation which tried to incorporate the British trade unions into the state, but merely alienated them. Heath also wanted the British bankers to become more like their German counterparts, taking direct stakes in British manufacturing. Heath's only substantial biographer to date tells us:

'During 1972 and 1973 Heath became increasingly critical of what he saw as the unpatriotic caution of businessmen in the face of the opportunities which he believed the Government was creating for them... [he] used to lecture the banks on their national responsibility, urging them to *invest directly in industry like German banks...*'[10] (Emphasis added.)

The Treasury did its sums and found that entry into the EEC was going to be very expensive. It was bypassed by a Prime Minister bent on transforming the British economy and generating economic growth.

'Heath had no time for the Treasury's caution. He had always thought it lukewarm on Europe, and was now convinced that it systematically underestimated the benefits to be expected from joining the EEC. The 1972 Budget was framed in *opposition to the Treasury*, as a deliberately *European* policy to take Britain

12

into the Community at full stretch.'[11] (First emphasis added, second in the original.)

For Heath and the little group around him EEC entry was everything. The strategy was not just a 'dash for growth,' but an attempt to transform the British economy in preparation for EEC entry. Unfortunately, British capital was as unimpressed by the proposals as the trade unions had been, and chose not to follow the suggestions. (It is worth noting that Heath was willing to try to use the law to change industrial relations but he relied on exhortation with the financial sector.) One section of British capital in particular, the City of London, which Heath seems to have largely ignored, had other ideas and conned Heath into passing legislation which it wanted.

Wheelbarrow Days[12]

While Heath was dreaming of transforming Britain into a modern, European, manufacturing economy, the City of London had been growing in another direction. The big expansion of City power began in the late 1960s with the development of London as an off-shore base for American money fleeing restrictions and low interest rates imposed by successive Democratic governments. Charles Gordon, part of the management of one of the so-called 'fringe banks' in London during this period, commented later:

'The colonial expansion of overseas banks into London in the 1960s and 70s created a near ring-fenced, on-shore, unregulated lending activity, which was simply mind-boggling in its enormous size...'[13]

In the midst of this growth in the late 1960s the main British banks, the so-called clearing banks, were increasingly unhappy:

'...unpaid agents of the state, bearing a great part of the considerable administrative burden of implementing exchange controls, in the post-war years their lending activities were almost constantly restricted by government, and they were the main agents through which the authorities tried to enforce periodic credit squeezes.'[14]

Chafing under government restrictions, the big clearing banks had to watch: the growth of pension funds, unit trusts and building societies as rivals for domestic saving; the arrival in London of increasing numbers of

13

foreign banks; and the rise of the so-called secondary banks which began to grow in the spaces left by the centrally restricted clearers. The regulatory body for the City, the Bank of England, was also under pressure because much of this financial activity was beyond their existing powers so they set up a joint committee with the Treasury to come up with a solution to these difficulties.[15] In the bureaucratic game that ensued, the Bank of England outmanoeuvred the Treasury, producing its own scheme while the Treasury was still thinking about things. (This is called 'bouncing' your opponent.)[16] The Treasury was not happy about the Bank of England's proposals, believing (correctly, as it turned out) that they would produce inflation.[17]

Having 'bounced' the Treasury, the Bank of England then 'bounced' the new Conservative Government.

In what was called Competition and Credit Control (C&CC hereafter), the Bank proposed that there would be an end to limits on lending and interest rates alone would be used to 'control' credit in the economy. C&CC was adopted as government policy in September 1971, barely noticed by the media, the Labour Opposition or by Heath himself.[18]

Indeed, at the time hardly anyone outside the higher echelons of the City seems to have known what was going on. Edward du Cann was at a meeting of the 1922 Committee of the Conservative Party at which the C&CC proposals were described:

> 'I looked round the room and wondered how many of the MPs present fully comprehended what he was talking about. I doubt whether more than half a dozen had the least idea.'[19]

The proposals had been whisked through the House of Commons in Chancellor Barber's budget speech. *The Economist* commented at the time:

> '...they had not been the subject of a single clause of legislation. Parliament has barely discussed it. It has all been fixed up as a gentleman's agreement in private conclaves in the City.'[20]

A contemporaneous account of C&CC, returning to Heath's desire to see more direct involvement by the British banks in industry, appeared in *The Economist* of 18 September 1971, 'The Banking Revolution.' This presented the consequences of C&CC as being a move towards:

> '...the German-Japanese system of largely bank-controlled industry...a situation in which banking would have even

14

greater control over British industry and the economy as a whole - that is, direct control through ownership and participation, rather than the indirect control it has exerted traditionally via government and the state.'

This was nonsense, disinformation. This may express what Heath sought but says nothing about the C&CC proposals. C&CC was simply the old order being reimposed on the British economy. This was the climax of all those attempts since the post-war era to get rid of government controls on banking. Under the new system the banks could lend what they liked and, when it was decided that there was too much credit in the system, they would put their interest rates up. It was a truly wonderful racket!

Having persuaded the Tories to reintroduce 'freedom' into the banking business, the clearing banks began generating credit (literally 'printing money'). They did not lend it to, or invest it in, British manufacturing as Heath seems to have expected, but to domestic consumers, to the property markets and the so-called 'fringe banks' (which in turn lent it on again, largely into property speculation).[21]

Charles Gordon, then with the secondary bank Cedar Holdings, described the period:

> 'These immediate years after C&CC were wonderful shovelling times. The main thrust of the banks (there were a number of honourable exceptions) was to apply the shovel with gusto not with discretion, lip-service was mouthed to the authorities, consequences were ignored, and pious condemnations were made of those who were found out patently overdoing it. Old-fashioned lending practices were contaminated, most of the lending industry was embroiled - from the newly liberated primary banks to the reeking sewage level of the tertiary lenders.'[22]

In the absence of any reference to this in his memoir, we don't know what Heath thought C&CC would do, if he thought anything at all. My guess would be that it was linked in his mind with the approaching entry into the EEC. As EEC entry was going to put up food prices and have other negative effects on the economy, Heath seems to have wanted to generate a head of steam in the domestic economy which would compensate for those effects.[23] I would guess that the Bank of England presented it to him along these lines. According to the creator of Trafalgar House Investments, Nigel Broackes, who dined with Heath in January 1972,

Heath said he 'wanted an investment boom with an abundance of cheap credit.'[24] He certainly presided over the making of a boom, cutting personal taxes, allowing interest on bank loans to be offset against tax and tripling the Public Sector Borrowing Requirement (PSBR) between 1971/2 and 1972/3.[25] But he didn't get the investment. Instead he got an inflationary domestic boom: credit exploded; consumer spending rose; and property prices rose. Consequently, so did imports. The balance of payments went into deficit, putting severe pressure on the value of the pound. Previous Prime Ministers in this situation would have tried to throttle the boom, reduce government spending and reduce consumer spending by making borrowing money more expensive. Heath did none of these. Rather than slow the boom he let the pound 'float,' preferring to see a falling pound rather than a slowing economy. What he got was roaring inflation.

Heath's gamble on a 'dash for growth' to kick-start Britain out of its stagnation failed. With little commercial and no industrial experience, Heath simply did not understand the British economy. Given the right expansionist conditions, Heath believed, British capitalism would increase investment in the domestic manufacturing economy. But it didn't, in part because for the previous fifteen years the British economy had been subject to periodic bouts of expansion which were always followed by contraction. This policy was derided as 'stop-go' by the Labour Party of the 1960s and discussed in many books analysing Britain's relative economic failure in the late 1950s and 1960s.[26] Why invest for the future if the rug was going to be pulled out a year or two down the line?

Heath took to berating those he thought should be investing, i.e. bankers, as we have seen already, and those running the big British companies. Head of the Confederation of British Industry (CBI), Sir Campbell Adamson said:

> 'I couldn't count on the fingers of both hands the number of times that Mr Heath told us that everything had been put right that the government could put right, and still industry didn't invest enough.'[27]

Heath sought an investment boom in Britain via cheap, plentiful credit but had allowed the introduction of a system, C&CC, which explicitly promised increases in interest rates to 'control' the supply of credit. In the event, when he belatedly realised what the C&CC changes entailed, Heath would not let the system work the way it was supposed to. The theory was that as people borrowed more the interest rates went up. But Heath refused to allow the rates to rise as far and as fast as the monetary experts at the

Bank of England wanted.[28] The result was the worst of all possible inflationary worlds - banks printing money day and night with low interest rates. Robert Heller and Norris Willatt noted:

> 'What had been created, under the eyes of the Bank of England, was a simulacrum of the lethally unbalanced Wall Street of the late and roaring twenties... between mid-1970 and early 1974 M3 (currency, current bank accounts and deposit accounts) rose by the previously unthinkable amount of 270%...'[29]

William Keegan points out that C&CC became a part of the 'dash for growth' when Chancellor Anthony Barber made bank loans tax deductible for many purposes, including the purchase of homes, second homes and shares, encouraging what was then 'the biggest credit binge in British post-war history.'[30]

Eventually, Heath began to realise it had all gone wrong and tried to reverse some of the changes. At the end of 1973, with the energy crisis (caused by the tripling of the price of oil) in full swing and the balance of payments deep in deficit, the brakes were slammed on the economy. Government spending was cut, surtax was increased, hire purchase controls were reintroduced and the 1971 C&CC reforms were virtually suspended.

But it was too late and, for the secondary banking and property sectors, it was too much.[31] The edifice of speculation, based on rising property and land prices, began to topple. By early 1974 inflation in Conservative Britain was heading for 20%, with more in the pipeline, and the Bank of England was forced to assemble financial assistance for the stricken moneylenders among the so-called secondary bankers.[32] The bankers had been given their heads and, with a good deal of help from the government, had made a complete bollocks of it.

Notes

1. 'The centrality of Europe to the administration's agenda was reflected in the establishment of a European Secretariat in the Cabinet Office.' Stuart Ball and Anthony Seldon, *The Heath Government 1970-74* (London: Longman, 1996), page 63.

2. John Campbell, *Edward Heath* (London: Jonathan Cape, 1993), page 452.

3. Campbell (see note 2), page 442.

4. 'The free-marketeers among the ministers at the Department of Trade and Industry knew nothing about it [the committee] despite the detailed Industry Bill which was to emerge.' Peter Hennessy, *Whitehall* (London: Secker and Warburg, 1989), page 239.

5. Campbell (see note 2), page 444. Pliatzky later said of this committee: 'The concept was that we must strengthen our industrial capacity so as to take advantage of membership of the Common Market.' Phillip Whitehead, *The Writing On The Wall: Britain In The Seventies* (London: Michael Joseph, 1985), page 82.

6. Department of Trade and Industry (DTI) Minister, Christopher Chataway, has confirmed that EEC membership was the rationale put forward by civil servants in the DTI for the Industry Bill. See Chataway's comments in Michael David Kandiah (ed), 'The Heath Government: A Witness Seminar,' *Contemporary Record*, Vol. 9, No.1, 1995, page 198.

7. Ball and Seldon (see note 1), page 40.

8. 'The origins of the incomes policy of autumn 1972, according to one insider who was closely involved, can be traced to "the early summer of 1972 when William Armstrong asked Ted Heath if we could start preparing contingency plans for a new counter-inflation strategy in case inflation topped 10%."' Hennessy (see note 4), page 231.

9. 'Heath had been very impressed, when visiting Germany, by Willy Brandt's regular round-table consultations with the unions and the German system of co-partnership; his mind began moving towards establishing a similar relationship in Britain by which the unions should be given an acknowledged role in the running of the economy.' Campbell (see note 2), page 444.

10. Campbell (see note 2), page 526.

11. Campbell (see note 2), page 444. See also Michael David Kandiah (ed), 'The Heath Government: A Witness Seminar' (see note 6).

12. 'Just take your wheelbarrow to the banks and cart away the cash' - Edward du Cann on the credit explosion after the introduction of the Com-

petition and Credit Control proposals of the Bank of England were introduced in 1971. Du Cann was then chair of the merchant bank Keyser Ullman. Edward du Cann, *Two Lives* (Upton on Severn: Images Publishing, 1995), page 131.

13. Charles Gordon, *The Cedar Story* (London: Sinclair-Stevenson, 1993), page 152. Gordon was then running Cedar Trust, which became one of the first casualties of the secondary banking crisis of 1973/4.

14. Michael Moran, 'Finance Capital And Pressure Group Politics In Britain,' *The British Journal Of Political Science*, Volume 11, 1981, page 396.

15. A very clear account of this is in Margaret Reid, *The Secondary Banking Crisis 1973-5* (London: Macmillan, 1982), chapter 3.

16. '...the Bank bounced the Treasury; produced its own scheme in the autumn of 1970 while the Allen committee was still pondering various options in a leisurely way.' Michael Moran, *The Politics Of Banking* (London: Macmillan, 1986), page 52. 'Bounce' is a term used in British political circles to describe the process by which a proposal is presented to an individual or committee in such a way as to ensure its approval without adequate discussion. In America the nearest equivalent would be 'end run.'

17. Reid (see note 15), pages 32/3.

18. John Campbell, Heath's only substantial biographer to date, gives C&CC a brief mention on page 455 (see note 2), and it is not referred to in Heath's 1998 memoir. The Bank of England's anodyne account of the changes was in a consultative document issued on 14 May 1971 and reproduced in the *Bank Of England Quarterly Bulletin*, June 1971, pages 181-193. The best discussion of C&CC is in Moran's *The Politics Of Banking* (see note 16).

19. Du Cann (see note 12), page 130.

20. 'The Banking Revolution,' *The Economist*, 18 September 1971.

21. Having complained about the activities of 'the fringe,' after C&CC the clearing banks threw money at them, playing a central role in the ensuing collapse.

22. Gordon (see note 13), page 149. This chapter on the post-C&CC fiasco is aptly titled 'Borrow Short, Lend Long And Go Bust.'

23. 'The Prime Minister also wanted to see Britain's industry in better competitive shape before the country joined the EEC on 1 January 1973.' Reid (see note 15), page 70.

24. Reid (see note 15), page 71.

25. The PSBR was money borrowed by the state from the financial sector and spent in the public sector. In other words, the government began spending more.

26. Of which the most famous was Michael Shanks, *The Stagnant Society* (Harmondsworth: Penguin, 1961).

27. Whitehead (see note 5), page 81. Similar anecdotal evidence is on Campbell (see note 2), page 526. Heath was trying to go in contradictory directions. On the one hand he was trying to take the unions into a tripartite management of the domestic economy. On the other, he was attacking them (as they saw it) with his industrial relations legislation.

28. 'The first serious efforts to allow interest rates to rise after 1971 produced a powerful reassertion of influence by those sensitive to the demands of industrial investors and mortgages in the housing market.' Moran (see note 16), pages 52/3.

29. Robert Heller and Norris Willatt, *Can You Trust Your Bank?* (London: Weidenfeld and Nicolson, 1977), page 102.

30. William Keegan, *Mrs Thatcher's Economic Experiment* (Harmondsworth: Penguin, 1985), pages 55/6. 'Between December 1971 and December 1974 the total assets of British banks rose from £36,865 million to £85,204 million - a rise of £48,339 million or 131 percent.' Douglas Jay, *Sterling: A Plea For Moderation* (London: Sidgwick and Jackson, 1985), page 148.

31. This view is expressed very strongly by Edward du Cann, then Chairman of the merchant bank Keyser Ullman, in his account of the crisis in his memoir *Two Lives*. See note 12.

32. The so-called Bank of England 'lifeboat.' Teresa Gorman MP, one of the 'radical right' group of Tory MPs who supported Mrs Thatcher, first entered politics in 1974, standing as a business-sponsored, independent, anti-Conservative candidate, in protest at the Heath government's 20% inflation. Teresa Gorman, *The Bastards* (London: Pan, 1993), pages 162/3.

2. 1976 And All That

After a series of protracted industrial disputes, notably with the National Union of Miners in 1973/4, Conservative Prime Minister Edward Heath called and lost an election in March 1974. Labour took office with no majority, called another election later that year and got an overall majority of only 4. It might have been a good election to lose, for Labour inherited the roaring inflation caused by the Heath Government *and* the worst balance of payments figures since the war.[1]

At this distance, the Labour Government of 1974-76 led by Harold Wilson looks like an unremarkable, mainstream, social democratic administration, mired in economic problems not of its own making. But a section of the British secret state and its allies in the Conservative Party, business and the media believed, or found it politically useful to *pretend* to believe, that British democracy, the state and even the capitalist system were under threat from a resurgent British left, spearheaded by the trade unions and manipulated by the British Communist Party under instruction from Moscow.[2] The fact that none of this manifested itself via the ballot box (the Communist Party received just 0.1% of the vote in the 1974 elections) did not matter.[3] A secret Communist conspiracy was, by definition, secret.

While Tony Benn was the chief focus of the paranoid right's conspiracy fantasies at parliamentary level, the Labour Cabinet was also regarded with suspicion and during this period many of its members, notably Wilson himself, were subjected to surveillance, burglaries and disinformation. The anti-Communist hysteria caused the formation of private armies by former intelligence and military personnel, media speculation on the right circumstances for Army intervention in Britain and a wide range of psyops, black bag jobs and disinformation projects.[4] A considerable chunk of the British establishment, including Heath's Cabinet Secretary, was in the grip of a ludicrous conspiracy theory about the Labour Party. Sean Stewart, who in 1975 was working for right-wing, pro-American Labour Cabinet member Peter Shore, commented later: 'Peter Shore was my minister: most of my colleagues thought he was a "fellow traveller"; and Benn was regarded as a Communist.'[5]

If this paranoia about the left was the background, in the foreground was the inflation generated during the Heath years, which reached 27% a year according to some accounts. The City/Treasury/Bank of England financial nexus did not think the Wilson Government was showing sufficient zeal to deflate the economy so they pushed on two fronts. In 1975 they tried, and failed, to impose a statutory wage control policy on the Wilson Government. In 1976 they tried, and failed, to impose massive public spending cuts. Both events contained the same features: demands from the financial sector; political games; and covert operations by sections of the Treasury.

'A Veritable Cornucopia Of Coincidence'[6]

In June 1975 inflation was at 27% and, according to Denis Healey who was Chancellor at the time, 'basic hourly rates were up 32% on the year.' This was the peak of the inflation *mostly* generated by the Heath Government and the peak of the worst economic crisis since the end of World War Two. For a Labour Government this presented a peculiarly difficult problem. The key to defeating inflation was then perceived to be controlling wage increases. The theory said that wage costs put up manufacturing costs which were passed on to consumers by price rises. But an employee getting a pay rise less than the cost of living increase (inflation) is taking a cut in their living standards. This was the nub: how would a party of the urban working class and trade union movement enforce a reduction in the living standards of its constituents? Accepting that it had to be done, Wilson was determined not to make the mistakes the Heath Government had made in seeking a statutory pay policy which would drive him into a head-on conflict with the unions. It was decided that Labour's pay policy would not be legally enforceable and it would have to include the miners (Heath's hadn't). Getting the miners' approval for such a pay policy, Wilson believed, could only be achieved at the miners' annual conference in July 1975. The Labour Government played for time until July but under pressure from what Wilson called:

> '...the bailiffs, in the shape of the international financial community, from cautious treasurers of international corporations, multinationals, to currency operators and monetary speculators.'[7]

Would they wait for Wilson's 'D-day in the battle against inflation' at the miners' annual conference? Bernard (now Lord) Donoughue was then head of the Downing Street Policy Unit, and he:

> '...learned from contacts in the Treasury that it had been decided to get the voluntary [pay policy] proposals rejected and to "bounce" a statutory policy through Ministers.'[8]

Donoughue informed Wilson of this attempted covert implementation of Treasury policy and Wilson then:

> '...dispatched to the Treasury what is the most commanding document ever sent in British Government - a Prime Minister's minute. This...gave blunt instructions not to proceed further with arguments for a statutory policy and to start analysing and constructing a voluntary policy along the lines already supported in [Cabinet committee] MISC 91... *The Treasury ignored the Prime Minister's instructions*.'[9] (Emphasis added.)

On Friday 27 June, Wilson predicted to both Joe Haines, his Press Secretary, and Donoughue that the Governor of the Bank of England or a senior official from the Treasury would appear on Monday, tell him that the pound was about to collapse and that drastic measures needed to be taken.[10]

On Monday 30 June, a wave of selling of Sterling took place; Sterling suffered its biggest fall in a day. As Wilson had predicted, the Governor of the Bank of England duly turned up on Monday at 2.45 p.m., declared that Sterling was collapsing and urged the Prime Minister to support the Chancellor, Denis Healey, in his proposals for a statutory incomes policy. The inner cabinet committee dealing with this issue, MISC 91, met that evening.

> 'At midnight, as the dinner guests were departing, the inevitable Treasury memorandum "bounced" into No.10. It...contained a totally stark statement of a statutory 10% pay policy, with criminal sanctions.'[11]

Joe Haines sat down and wrote Wilson a memorandum which began:

> 'We believe that the Cabinet are being faced with an attempt by the Treasury to stampede it into a statutory pay policy, against every pledge which we have given.'[12]

Joe Haines commented later:

> 'Bernard Donoughue and I were suspicious about the sudden run on the pound so quickly after the Prime Minister's minute on the previous Friday... There was one further piece of evidence which had come to us during the evening which strengthened our suspicions about the behaviour of the Treasury. No attempt had been made by the Bank of England to

keep the pound above the crucial $2.20 level. No money had been spent to bolster the rate...[it was] a veritable cornucopia of coincidence.'[13]

But the Treasury/Bank of England manoeuvres failed. The Labour Cabinet did not implement an incomes policy 'backed by criminal sanctions' against employees and, oddly enough, the pound did not 'go.'

The IMF Incident

Through the rest of 1975 and into 1976 the situation remained the same. Formally floating, the pound was under constant downwards pressure because British inflation was higher than that of other industrialised countries. Its value was being defended by the Bank of England. Seeking to bring inflation down without a major recession (which Mrs Thatcher was to create in 1980-3) or the massive industrial trouble which had helped end the Heath Government, the Labour Government sought a voluntary incomes policy which would stick. Having failed to force a statutory incomes policy on the Government, the financial nexus sought a reduction in Government borrowing and spending. (If wages were not going to be cut sufficiently to maintain the pound at the level the financial sector wanted, they would enforce a reduction in consumption of publicly provided goods and services.) Eventually the Government, now led by James Callaghan, after Wilson's resignation in 1976, decided to go to the International Monetary Fund (IMF) to borrow money with which to defend the value of the pound.

'We had the feeling it could really come apart in quite a serious way...so we tended to see it [the IMF incident] in cosmic terms' - William Rogers, US Secretary of State

The IMF incident is well documented and hardly needs rehashing here in detail.[14] On one side there was the US financial administration, the Conservative Party, most of the media and some of the financial nexus who wanted the IMF to impose its traditional policy prescriptions (deflation, in one form or another, which would mean cuts and unemployment) as a condition of a loan with which to support the value of Sterling. On the other side, the Labour Government wanted the loan but tried to evade, as far as possible, the deflationary conditions which would accompany it. A prolonged game of chicken was played out. Using the prospect of possible economic chaos, damage to NATO (British troop withdrawal from West

24

Germany was talked of at one point) and the threat from the British left, members of the Labour Cabinet, notably Prime Minister Callaghan and Harold Lever, tried to mobilise political support within the US Government and the NATO alliance against the US Treasury and IMF officials who wished to impose a severe deflationary package on the Labour Government.

The struggle with the IMF centred around the projected Public Sector Borrowing Requirement (PSBR), which is the level of proposed Government borrowing. The bigger the projected PSBR, the bigger the cuts in Government spending the IMF would demand. The Treasury helped create the sense of crisis six months before, in February 1976, by issuing false figures on public spending which apparently showed that it was taking 60% of Britain's Gross Domestic Product.[15] The true figure was 46%. The Treasury rigged the figures to make life difficult for the Government (by that stage an approach to the IMF was being discussed). A similar move was made during the early stages of negotiations with the IMF. The Treasury's grossly exaggerated estimate of the PSBR for 1977/8 was leaked to the *Financial Times*.[16]

Conspiracy

Members of the Callaghan Government knew their opponents were working against them. Prime Minister Callaghan,[17] Liberal MP John Pardoe[18] and *Guardian* journalist Peter Jenkins reported being warned of a US/UK financial conspiracy against the Government.[19] Callaghan's advisor, Bernard Donoughue:

> '...was privately summoned to the United States Embassy for a secret meeting with a very senior official there who said, "You should be aware of something, which is that parts of the Treasury are in very deep cahoots with parts of the US Treasury and with certain others in Germany who are of very right-wing inclination and they are absolutely committed to getting the IMF here and if it brings about the break-up of this Government, they will be very, very happy." He actually showed me a copy of a secret communication between London and Washington which seemed to confirm this view.'[20]

In his book *Prime Minister*, Donoughue commented:

'We were not being paranoid in 1976 in our suspicion that the IMF was capable of launching economic "remedies" which would destroy Governments (especially Governments of the left). A year later in November 1977 the IMF mission to Portugal (including a senior member of the 1976 mission to the UK) refused to grant a credit tranche to the socialist minority Government led by Mr Soares because he would not make immediate savage economies, which would certainly have brought down his administration and allowed back into power the old anti-Democratic parties of the far right. An internal IMF briefing, which we saw among diplomatic papers in Downing Street at that time, stated quite brutally that *the IMF policy was to create a foreign exchange crisis* over the next two months. The IMF staff explicitly asked the Western Governments of the United States, Germany, Japan and Britain to withhold financial and economic aid in order to create a foreign exchange crisis which would bring the Soares Government to its knees and so force it to accept the harsh IMF prescription.'[21] (Emphasis added.)

At the end of all the wrangles, the weeks of cabinet debate, the international horse-trading and arm-twisting, and the disinformation from within the financial nexus in Britain, the result was a victory for the Prime Minister and the politicians over the international financial officials. Accepting the need for a deal with the IMF, if only for the IMF 'seal of approval' to display to the financial markets, Callaghan used the NATO alliance dimension to greatly reduce the conditions on the loan.

Defeated again, the Treasury faction which wanted the IMF to teach the Government a harsh lesson made a final attempt to deceive it. In the Prime Minister's Policy Unit, Bernard Donoughue was monitoring the conclusion of the IMF negotiations. The focus of his interest was the Letter of Intent, which is the contract between the Government and the IMF. After some trouble getting hold of a copy, Donoughue found the contract and discovered the agreed figures had been changed to make life more difficult for the Government.[22]

The IMF incident is a major feature of both left and right beliefs about the 1970s.

For the Conservatives it is a symbol of Labour economic incompetence and national humiliation. But this view conveniently forgets that it was

Conservative policies which created the mess in the first place. For the Labour left it became a potent symbol of betrayal and sell-out to international capitalism. But this view ignores the political reality of the time. After the first 1974 election Labour had only four more seats than the Conservatives and no overall majority. After the second 1974 election there was an overall majority of four which was whittled away by death and by-elections. Between 1974 and 1979 the Labour Party was kept in office by the minor parties, chiefly the Liberals. It received less than 40% of the votes cast in both elections. Those on the Labour left, from Tony Benn down, who believed the Labour Governments of 1974-79 should have and could have acted more radically than they did, seem strangely oblivious to these elementary electoral facts. There really was little choice. The left did not have the political support in Cabinet, in Parliament or among the electorate, for the radical alternatives they offered.

The actual significance of the 'crisis' in 1976 can be judged by the fact that the cuts finally required by the IMF were all quietly restored by the Government the following year. Only half the IMF loan was used and the rest was repaid without incident. Six months after the IMF team flew back to Washington the problem with the pound was not that it was falling too far (the reason the IMF was approached in the first place) but that it was rising too fast because the financial speculators began to factor the approaching revenues from North Sea oil into their calculations. The uncomfortable truth for both left and right is that in 1979 the Callaghan Government was succeeding in its central aim: bringing inflation down without creating a major recession. This does not sit properly with both left and right myths about the period.

At the end of the 1970s, after nearly a decade of economic problems caused by inflation, sections of the Conservative and Labour Parties were in the grip of betrayal myths about their own leaders. The group around Tory leader Margaret Thatcher believed that the Heath Government had betrayed true Toryism and/or the British nation state. The Labour left believed that the Callaghan Government had betrayed socialism/the working class/the true Labour Party. The Thatcher group had taken over the Conservative Party; and the Labour left seemed on the verge of taking over Labour.

The economic problems caused by the hyper-inflation of the mid-1970s cost Labour the 1979 election. Labour was blamed for the inflation of the preceding five years, even though it had been created by the Heath Government, and for the strikes and disruption of the so-called 'Winter of Discontent' of 1978/9 during which the trade unions responded to the

Callaghan Government's attempts to reduce inflation by cutting their members' wages. The brothers Saatchi came up with their notorious 'Labour Isn't Working' posters in which Conservative Party employees pretended to be a dole queue. A vote for the Conservatives, apparently, would reduce unemployment. That this was an obvious nonsense counted for nothing. Mrs Thatcher proposed to reduce unemployment by reducing inflation, but her proposed cure for inflation, monetarism, guaranteed and depended upon increasing unemployment. The Callaghan Government was turned out of office in favour of a Government whose central policies promised to do the same as its predecessor, only more so!

The belief that the key to controlling inflation was by controlling the money supply was used by a small group, led by Keith Joseph, as the stick with which to beat Ted Heath. Heath, they perceived correctly, was chiefly responsible for the inflation. (It is impossible to exaggerate the horror with which that inflation was perceived by orthodox Tories.) Monetarism amounted to little more than a pseudo-scientific rationale for creating a big recession. The traditional solution to inflation had always been to deflate the economy, i.e. put some of the workers on the dole and close some businesses.

Thatcher had also been seriously infected by conspiracy theories about the Labour Party and trade unions being in the grip of the KGB. These theories had been coming from the anti-subversive right for the previous decade.[23] She had been tutored in this by no less a person than Brian Crozier, doyen of the subversive-hunters.[24] She took this nonsense as far as putting her suspicions that Harold Wilson was a KGB agent(!) to Robert Armstrong, then No.2 at the Home Office and the liaison with MI5. She had three meetings with Armstrong on this subject in 1977.[25] For Mrs Thatcher, the recession prescribed by her dimly-perceived theories about the money supply had the welcome effect of punishing the enemy within, i.e. the labour movement and the industrial working class, with unemployment.

Mrs Thatcher wanted to fight the Cold War at home and abroad and restore 'sound money.' These were fine orthodox Tory views of a certain ilk. It was Britain's tragedy that the Thatcher faction took office in 1979 bent on causing a recession which, even in orthodox terms, the economy didn't need because the outgoing Labour Government had been successfully bringing inflation down slowly, trying to minimise the damage to the economy. In effect, although dressed up as monetarism, Mrs Thatcher and her little band imposed the big recession on the economy that the International Monetary Fund had sought in 1976.

Labour Commits Suicide?

The received version of the Labour Party's history in this period is that the left: took over the party and chose Michael Foot as its leader (despite his role in the Callaghan Government); imposed its agenda on the party; wrote the manifesto for the 1983 election (what Gerald Kaufman MP called 'the longest suicide note in history'); and was decisively rejected at the General Election in 1983. This is true up to a point. However, there are a number of caveats here which, though they may seem banal, are necessary. The most obvious is that had it not been for the Falklands War, Mrs Thatcher would have been turned out of office in 1983, 'the longest suicide note in history' notwithstanding. Up until the war, she was the most unpopular Prime Minister of the post-war era. Also, the Tories might have lost in 1983 if the Social Democratic Party (SDP) had not been formed in 1981. Even with the advantage of having won a war, the Conservatives only received 12,991,000 votes at the 1983 General Election, while their opponents received 16,212,000. The massive Tory majority of 144 in 1983 was actually achieved with 1% fewer votes that they received in 1979.

Happily for the Conservatives, their opponents were divided. Labour received 8,437,000 votes, the party's lowest vote ever recorded, and the Liberal/Democrat Alliance (the Social Democratic Party plus Liberals) received 7,775,000. However, thanks to the idiosyncrasies of the first-past-the-post electoral system, Labour had 209 seats and the Alliance only 23.

The formation of the SDP was critical to both the Labour Party and the Thatcher clique in the Tory Party, and it is the American tendency within Labour who must be examined next.

Notes

1. How much of the inflation of this period was directly attributable to the activities of the banks is impossible to quantify. In this period there was some wage inflationary pressure from the British trade unions, demand pressure in the domestic economy from the Government's increase in the Public Sector Borrowing Requirement in 1972/3 and 1973/4, the 1973 increase in the price of oil, rises in other commodities and the rise in food prices resulting from entry into the EEC and membership of the Common Agricultural Policy. This last point, generally ignored, is made by Douglas Jay in his *Sterling: A Plea For Moderation* (London: Sidgwick and Jackson, 1985), pages 155/6.

2. A good example of the theory is the full page article 'Communists Aim To Dictate Labour Policy,' *The Daily Telegraph*, 28 January 1974.

3. Figures from David Butler and Dennis Kavanagh, *The British General Election Of October 1974* (London: Macmillan, 1975), page 294.

4. This period is discussed in detail in Stephen Dorril and Robin Ramsay, *Smear! Wilson And The Secret State* (London: Fourth Estate, 1991), chapters 34-39.

5. Roger Broad and Tim Geiger (eds), 'The 1975 British Referendum On Europe: A Witness Seminar,' *Contemporary Record* Vol. 10, No.3, 1996, page 103.

6. Joe Haines, *The Politics Of Power* (London: Jonathan Cape, 1977), page 59.

7. Harold Wilson, *Final Term: The Labour Government 1974-76* (London: Weidenfeld and Nicolson, 1979), page 114.

8. Bernard Donoughue, *Prime Minister: The Conduct Of Policy Under Harold Wilson And James Callaghan* (London: Jonathan Cape, 1987), page 66. The word 'bounce' is used to partially conceal or underplay what is being described, i.e. an unelected group of civil servants are trying to impose their views on the Government.

9. Donoughue (see note 8), page 66.

10. Haines (see note 6), page 50; Donoughue (see note 8), page 66.

11. Donoughue (see note 8), page 68.

12. Haines (see note 6), page 59.

13. Haines (see note 6), pages 58/9.

14. A recent thorough, albeit conventional, re-examination is Kathleen Burk and Alec Cairncross, *Goodbye Great Britain: The 1976 IMF Crisis* (London: Yale University Press, 1992).

15. Denis Healey, *The Time Of My Life* (London: Michael Joseph, 1989), page 42.

16. Burk and Cairncross (see note 14), page 70.

17. James Callaghan, *Time And Chance* (London: Collins, 1987), page 43.

18. Ken Coates (ed), *What Went Wrong?* (Nottingham: Spokesman, 1979), page 182.

19. Cited in Haines (see note 6), page 58.

20. Symposium on the 1976 IMF crisis in *Contemporary Record,* Vol. 3, No.2, November 1989, page 43.

21. Donoughue (see note 8), pages 95/6.

22. Donoughue (see note 8), pages 99/100. There are other versions of the same events in Phillip Whitehead, *The Writing On The Wall: Britain In The Seventies* (London: Michael Joseph, 1985), page 199 and Burk and Cairncross (see note 14), page 107.

23. During her years in office the only novel she was ever reported as reading (and rereading) was Frederick Forsyth's *The Fourth Protocol* whose central theme, handily put in italics, is that the KGB controlled the Labour Party and any Labour Government, no matter how 'moderate' it appeared, would be overthrown by an internal coup and replaced by the hard left. Mrs Thatcher, it may now be acknowledged, was rather dim.

24. On Crozier and Thatcher see Brian Crozier, *Free Agent* (London: HarperCollins, 1993), chapter 10.

25. See Kenneth O Morgan, *Callaghan: A Life* (Oxford: Oxford University Press, 1997), page 610.

3. The American Tendency
In The Labour Party

There has been what we might call an American tendency within the Labour Party since the end of World War Two. As is now well documented, during the Cold War the US tried, with considerable success, to regulate the entire non-Communist world by making it open its doors to American capital, allow American military bases and accept American political leadership.[1]

In 1945 the USA was in a position of unparalleled power. Undamaged by the war, it was producing something like half the world's economic wealth. After the war, it created a large propaganda and intelligence operation in Western Europe which accompanied dollar loans and American goods into the war-ravaged European economies.[2] If you wanted the dollars and the goodies, you had to get on the programme.

In the British Labour Party this entailed sending large numbers of trade unionists and Labour politicians on 'freebies' to the United States to see how wonderful the place was. Among the American tendency in the Parliamentary Labour Party who made visits were party leader Hugh Gaitskell, his deputy George Brown, Anthony Crosland and Douglas Jay.[3] In one programme alone, the Anglo-American Council on Productivity, 900 people from Britain (managers and union officials), went on trips to the United States.[4] Hundreds of trade union officers visited the US in the 1950s under the auspices of the European Productivity Agency, and groups of British union leaders were sent on a three-month trade union programme run by the Harvard Business School.[5]

Working out of the US Embassy was the Labour Attaché programme, which was established towards the end of the war. In the words of one of its creators, Philip Kaiser:

> 'The labor attaché is expected to develop contacts with key leaders in the trade union movement, and to influence their thinking and decisions in directions *compatible with American goals*.'[6] (Emphasis added.)

The first US Labour Attaché in London was Sam Berger who, according to Denis Healey, 'exerted an enduring influence on British foreign policy.'[7] There were also Labour Information Officers attached to the Marshall Plan staff in the US Embassy in London who promoted the American tendency within the British Labour movement.[8] Eventually Joe

Godson, Labour Attaché in London from 1953-59, helped Labour Party leader Gaitskell devise Labour Party policies and plan campaigns against the Labour left.[9]

There was a Europeanwide programme to boost the social democratic wings of socialist parties and movements. The biggest of these programmes was a CIA operation called the Congress for Cultural Freedom (CCF) which promoted the British social democrats - the American tendency in Labour. The CCF organised large conferences all over the world and began publishing journals, e.g. *Encounter* first appeared in Britain in 1953. *Encounter* became a major outlet for the 'revisionist,' i.e. pro-American, thinking of the younger intellectuals around Labour leader Hugh Gaitskell. These included Peter Jay, Patrick Gordon-Walker, Roy Jenkins and Anthony Crosland, all of whom were in Harold Wilson's first cabinet in 1964.[10]

I think it likely that in the 1950s Labour's American tendency believed that they and progressive, democratic forces (people they perceived to be like themselves) were taking part in a 'liberal conspiracy' (the title of Peter Coleman's study of the CCF) against the Soviet Union and its supporters. From the CIA's point of view, they were being run in a covert operation. The struggle against Stalinism was just one aim of the operation. The Americans also sponsored and funded the European social democrats because social democracy was a means of ensuring that the Governments of Europe continued to allow American capital into their economies with the minimum of restrictions. The US had no interest in democracy per se. For example, in Italy the Americans funded fascists and terrorists.[11]

After Labour's third successive election defeat in 1959, the American tendency began discussing changing the party's name, ditching the link with the trade unions, abandoning Clause 4 of the party's constitution and turning Labour into something resembling the American Democratic Party. None of this was practical at the time but all of it has since been done by the tendency's successors under Tony Blair. This American tendency in the Labour Party expected to take office eventually under its leader, Hugh Gaitskell, but when Gaitskell died suddenly the tendency was unable to agree upon a single leadership candidate. Instead, Harold Wilson became party leader, and then Prime Minister in 1964. Leadership of the American tendency was taken up by Roy Jenkins and, after seeing off the Campaign for Nuclear Disarmament's (CND) challenge to Labour policy on British nuclear weapons and US bases in Britain, the central issue for the tendency became achieving British entry into the European Economic Community (the EEC or 'Common Market').

European unity had been one of the projects favoured by the USA, which was looking for good anti-Soviet alliances during the Cold War, and the European Movement had been funded by the CIA.[12] Support for EEC membership within the Labour Party had first been formally organised in 1959 by the Labour Common Market Committee (co-founded by Roy Jenkins) which became the Labour Committee for Europe in the mid-1960s. In 1970 the election of the Heath Government meant that another serious effort to get Britain into the EEC would be made and the issue would divide the Labour Party then in opposition. On 10 October 1971, after a pro- and anti-EEC clash in the Shadow Cabinet, Tony Benn commented in his diary on the emergence of 'a European Social Democrat wing in the Parliamentary Party led by Bill Rodgers.'[13] (Rodgers had been the chief organiser of the American tendency's anti-CND group in the 1960s, called the Campaign for Democratic Socialism (CDS).) This group formally announced itself on 28 October, when 69 pro-EEC Labour MPs voted with the Conservative Government in favour of entry into the EEC in principle. From then on, the group operated as a party within a party, with Bill Rodgers acting as an unofficial whip.

From 1970 to 1973 various members of the American tendency within the Labour Party approached Roy Jenkins to leave Labour and start a new party. On each occasion Jenkins declined to do so.[14] In his memoir Jenkins describes 1975 as:

'...a great missed opportunity for Heath and [William] White-law and a whole regiment of discarded Conservative "wets" as much as for Shirley Williams and [David] Steel and me.'[15]

Jenkins was writing about the 1975 Common Market referendum campaign during which he found it more congenial working with pro-EEC Tories and Liberals than he did with the left wing of his own party. There is a large hint in Thatcher's second volume of memoirs that some kind of centrist realignment in British politics was attempted on the back of the referendum.[16] In 1976 Jenkins' participation was invited but once again he declined to act.[17]

When Harold Wilson resigned in 1976, Jenkins stood for leader of the Labour Party, lost (as he knew he would) and left British politics for Brussels as President of the EEC. In 1977 some of the pro-EEC American tendency group of MPs formed the Campaign for a Labour Victory. Alec McGivan, Bill Rodgers' PA, was one of the chief organisers and its full-time worker. Four years later he became the first full-time employee of the Social Democratic Party (SDP).

While Jenkins was in exile in Brussels, the American tendency began preparing for the new party. Two academics in London, Stephen Haseler and Douglas Eden, formed the Social Democratic Alliance (SDA) to fight the Labour left on the ground. From them emerged a string of alarmist reports about the inroads being made into the Labour Party by the left. The SDA attracted support from the union right and from other, surprising sources, including Brian Crozier, who was an MI6 and CIA asset, and a leading hunter of subversives.[18]

In November 1979, after Roy Jenkins had given the Dimbleby Lecture on BBC TV in which he more or less announced his intention of forming a social democratic party, businessman Clive Lindley and London Labour Councillor Jim Daley, both of whom had been active in the Campaign for Labour Victory, set up a support group for Jenkins.[19] Finally, a group met to discuss forming the new party: Stephen Haseler from the Social Democratic Alliance; Clive Lindley and Jim Daley from Roy Jenkins' UK support group; David Marquand, Jenkins' PA in Brussels; and Lord Harris, who had been Jenkins' PR man in the 1960s. This was the core of Jenkins' network plus Haseler.

The formation of the SDP in 1981, in the midst of the worst recession since the 1930s, probably ensured, and in my estimation was intended to ensure, that Labour would lose the next general election. Given the economic and social consequences for the UK of another decade of Conservative economic disaster, this must count as the most destructive action taken against the UK since World War Two.

To make certain Labour lost, members of the American tendency took other steps to ensure a Labour defeat. In 1980, after the decision had been taken by the Jenkins group to form a new party (but it had not been announced) there was a contest for the leadership of the Labour Party between Denis Healey of the centre-right coalition and Michael Foot of the centre-left coalition. Foot just about won, by the votes cast for him by seven Labour MPs *who subsequently defected to the Social Democratic Party*. Neville Sandelson, one of the seven, revealed this:

> 'Myself and my colleagues who voted for Foot were leaving the Labour Party and setting up a new party under the leadership of the Gang of Four and it was important that we finished off the job. It was very important that the Labour Party as it had become was *destroyed*.'[20] (Emphasis added.)

Some of the Labour right, who had not defected to the SDP and had just seen their candidate, Denis Healey, lose the leadership contest, then made sure the Labour Party had both a left-wing leader and a left-wing manifesto for the 1983 General Election. At the 1983 meeting between the Shadow Cabinet and Labour's National Executive Committee to finalise the manifesto for the forthcoming election, trade union leader John Golding, from what Roy Hattersley called 'the hard right,' proposed adopting all the policies being suggested by the left. This was carried with virtually no discussion. The usual left/right struggle over the manifesto, which Roy Hattersley had been anticipating, did not materialise. The right had decided that since they were going to lose the election anyway (the 'Falklands factor' and the formation of the SDP had ensured that) they would see that it was lost with all the left's policies attached to it.[21] Thus the 'takeover' of the Labour Party by the left (left leader and left election manifesto) was delivered by the right. As the old cliché has it, politics is a rough old game!

The Social Democratic Party was the 'coming out' of much of the American tendency in Labour. The leaders, the so-called Gang of Four (Roy Jenkins, Shirley Williams, David Owen and Bill Rodgers), had been career-long members of the American tendency in Labour. Fellow SDP founder Stephen Haseler worked in the 1980s for the American think-tank, the Heritage Institute, and was one of the founders (using Heritage money) of the Institute for European Defence and Strategic Studies, the London think-tank set up to challenge CND in the 1980s. In his review essay of the Crewe/King history of the SDP, Tom Easton noted some of the less well-known American connections to the party:

'The draft constitution of the new party was written in Massachusetts by two of the SDP's founders, Robert Maclennan and William Goodhart. Shirley Williams came straight to the critical prelaunch meeting of the Gang of Four from one of her regular Anglo-American conference get-togethers at Ditchley Park. When the party suddenly needed a new leader after [David] Owen's decision to go it alone, Williams met Maclennan in the United States to persuade him to take on the job.'

'Or again, when a decision was subsequently taken to merge with the Liberals, Maclennan tearfully insisted on membership of NATO being written into the constitution. And in the course of that merger one of the authors of the proposed joint policy statement was seconded to the job by his employer [CSIS], a propagandising Washington foreign policy think-tank much used by successive American administrations in pursuit of its foreign policy goals.'[22]

Quite soon after the formation of the SDP an article appeared in the magazine *The Leveller* titled 'The SDP And The CIA.' The authors presented little evidence of the CIA's role but their general suspicions were correct. The SDP was the American tendency with a great many links to American Government and quasi-Governmental organisations. As Tom Easton put it in his essay on the SDP's formation, the new party appeared at a time of great anxiety in Washington about the future loyalty of a number of European countries to the American-dominated international order. There were Europeanwide protests over the Reagan administration's cranking-up of the Cold War. (As usual, in the event of war breaking out, the Americans appeared intent on fighting the Soviet 'threat' down to the last European) So in 1981, in the depths of the Tory-created recession, it looked likely that Labour, complete with policies advocating unilateral nuclear disarmament, withdrawal from NATO and withdrawal from the EEC, was going to win the next election. There is no evidence as yet of American direction of the formation of the SDP but, for the Americans, the timing of their friends in Labour could hardly have been better.

Notes

1. This is too big a subject to document here but the following provide a way in: William Blum, *Killing Hope: US Military And CIA Interventions Since World War 2* (Monroe, Maine, USA: Common Courage Press, 1995) is the best single volume survey of known US military and paramilitary actions; Scott Lucas, *Freedom's War: The US Crusade Against The Soviet Union 1945-56* (Manchester, UK: Manchester University Press, 1999) goes into some of the areas in Blum's survey in greater detail; and Chalmers Johnson, *Blowback: The Costs And Consequences Of American Empire* (London: Little,Brown, 2000) discusses some of these events in the generally neglected Far East.

2. The best account of this is in Anthony Carew, *Labour Under The Marshall Plan* (Manchester, UK: Manchester University Press, 1987).

3. There is no detailed examination of this as far as I know and I don't know how many such programmes were run. Roy Hattersley commented that his first visit to the US was paid for by 'something which was laughingly called The Young Leaders' Program,' *The Guardian*, 27 February

1995. Mrs Thatcher made the same trip, in the same programme, in 1967. See her *Path To Power* (London: HarperCollins, 1995), page 153.

4. Carew (see note 2), page 137.

5. Carew (see note 2), pages 189/90.

6. Philip Kaiser, *Journeying Far And Wide* (Oxford: Maxwell Macmillan International, 1992), page 113. 'The labor attaché... had... an unusual opportunity to enhance American influence among individuals and institutions that historically have no contact with US diplomatic missions,' page 119.

7. Denis Healey, *The Time Of My Life* (London: Michael Joseph, 1989), page 113. Sam Berger has two innocuous entries in *The Diary Of Hugh Gaitskell 1945-56* (London: Jonathan Cape, 1983) and the footnote by editor Philip Williams on page 120 that he was 'first secretary at the US Embassy' conceals Berger's true role.

8. Carew (see note 2), pages 128/9

9. See Williams (ed) (see note 7). Godson's obituary is in *The Times*, 6 September 1986.

10. See Frances Stonor Saunders, *Who Paid The Piper? The CIA And The Cultural Cold War* (London: Granta Books, 1999) for the best extant account of the CCF. The 1955 CCF conference in Milan, 'The Future of Freedom,' was attended by Crosland, Richard Crossman, Denis Healey and Roy Jenkins. Labour Party leader Hugh Gaitskell attended the conferences in 1955, 1957, 1958 and 1962. Gaitskell, Jenkins, Anthony Crosland, Rita Hinden, Patrick Gordon-Walker, John Strachey and Dennis Healey were published in *Encounter*. See Peter Coleman, *The Liberal Conspiracy* (London: Collier Macmillan, 1989), pages 73, 100, 185. Crosland was a member of the International Council of the CCF. His role, said the CIA officer running CCF, was 'encouraging sympathetic people' to attend CCF conferences.

11. See Phillip Willan, *Puppet Masters: The Political Use Of Terrorism In Italy* (London: Constable, 1991).

12. The best account is Richard Aldrich, *The Hidden Hand: Britain, America And Cold War Secret Intelligence* (London: John Murray, 2001), chapter 16.

13. Tony Benn, *Office Without Power, Diaries 1968-72* (London: Arrow, 1988), page 381.

14. Ian Bradley, *Breaking The Mould? The Birth And Prospects Of The Social Democratic Party* (Oxford: Martin Robertson, 1981), pages 53-5.

15. Roy Jenkins, *A Life At The Centre* (London: Macmillan, 1991), page 426.

16. Margaret Thatcher, *Path To Power* (London: HarperCollins, 1995), page 331.

17. An account of some of this, from the diary of one of the participants, Labour MP Reg Prentice, is in Stephen Haseler, *The Battle For Britain* (London: Leo Cooper, 1994), pages 59/60.

18. Brian Crozier's memoir, *Free Agent* (London: HarperCollins, 1993) describes much of this.

19. Bradley (see note 14), page 73.

20. *The Sunday Telegraph*, 14 January 1996. This was actually revealed in Phillip Whitehead's study of the 1970s, *The Writing On The Wall* (London: Michael Joseph, 1985), page 359, but no one, including this writer, noticed its significance at the time.

21. Roy Hattersley told this story in 'Comrades At War,' part 2 of the series *The Wilderness Years*, BBC2, December 1995. He was told of the strategy by John Golding after the meeting.

22. This quotation is from the best short account of the SDP, Tom Easton's 'Who *Were* The SDP Travelling With?' in *Lobster* 31. Easton's essay included the following sources on Georgetown University and CSIS: Fred Landis, 'Georgetown's Ivory Tower For Old Spooks,' *Inquiry*, 30 September 1979; David Leigh, 'A Friend Of Taiwan: Ray Cline, A Scholar-Lobbyist, Wears Many Hats At Georgetown,' *Washington Post*, 29 June 1980; Alison Muscatine, 'Georgetown's Media Profs: A University Thinks Hard About Its Think Tank,' *Washington Post*, 11 May 1986; Jim McManus, 'Georgetown University Think Tank Lures Strategists, Military Contractors: President Ponders Its Future,' *National Catholic Reporter*, 3 October 1986.

4. Loadsamoney!

While all this party politicking and geo-politicking was going on, the City of London had control of Conservative economic policy and was getting rich.

The first Thatcher Government took office with one central economic ambition: they wanted to conquer inflation by 'controlling the money supply.' To do this they believed they had to do two things. First, reduce Government spending and borrowing. In practice this meant cutting back on state provision of public services. Second, they believed the supply of credit in the economy could be controlled by raising interest rates. In practice this meant creating a recession. Both were undertaken by the Thatcher Government. Implementation of the original IMF prescription for Britain in 1976 which was watered down by the Callaghan Government's campaign, was begun by the Thatcher Government three years later.

Raising interest rates and cutting Government spending may have been on the agenda of Thatcher and Chancellor of the Exchequer Geoffrey Howe (both of whom had been tax lawyers and knew little about economics), but the City of London had other agenda items and they could use their man in the Government to get them done. Their man was Howe's deputy, a former financial journalist named Nigel Lawson. The City wanted 'freedom' (that Tory buzzword of the time) and that meant the abolition of exchange controls and other restrictions on their activities. Unconcerned by the mess created by partial deregulation of the financial sector between 1971 and 1974, discussed above, the Thatcher Government between 1979 and 1982:

- Abolished exchange controls;

- Ended the restrictions on building society lending (starting them off on the road to becoming banks), thus beginning the great credit explosion of the later 1980s;

- Abolished the restrictions on bank lending which had been introduced by the previous Government;

- Abolished the Reserve Assets Ratio which made the banks hold at least 12.5% of their deposits in some specified range of liquid assets, thus enabling them to lend more;

- Abolished hire purchase restrictions.[1]

This was the rebirth of the Competition and Credit Control changes of 1971, with the additional abolition of exchange controls sought by a section of the financial nexus since the early 1950s.

At the top of this City shopping list was the abolition of exchange controls. Among the lobby for their abolition were 'most of the top people at the Bank of England, especially those responsible for administering exchange controls,'[2] Nigel Lawson[3] and Mrs Thatcher, who tells us in her memoirs that she 'took the greatest personal pleasure in [their] removal.'[4]

With interest rates raised and exchange controls abolished, so began the great Conservative recession of 1979-92, which led to two million unemployed and the great flight of capital from the UK. Looking back at this period the single most striking question is: why did the Government care so little about the collapse of British manufacturing? Why did it ignore the protests from its loyal supporters in British manufacturing as they went to the wall? Partly it was because some not very bright people were in the grip of theories. When the theories about controlling the money supply didn't seem to be working, they told themselves (and were told by their advisers) that it would take time for the medicine to cure the patient. They had to be 'tough' about things. Evoking Heath's 'betrayal,' Mrs Thatcher famously told her party's conference, "U-turn if you want to, the lady's not for turning." There was also another theory in the background which told them that manufacturing didn't really matter.

In 1999 Will Hutton, editor of *The Observer*, and one of the many people picked up and then discarded by the Blair faction, commented:

'The new intellectual and political consensus is that manufacturing no longer matters. The future is the knowledge economy and the service sector. Manufacturing is yesterday's story: very Old Labour, very uncool Britannia.'[5]

I think Hutton is correct that this is the current consensus in New Labour leadership circles *but it isn't new*. These attitudes first began to appear in the late 1970s when the scale of future North Sea oil production and revenues began to become clear. This appeared to present a difficulty, as follows:

1. As Britain produced more oil it would need to import less oil, eventually becoming self-sufficient. Assuming the British economy continued exporting as much as it had before oil, the result would be a growing trade *surplus*.

2. In the absence of measures to counteract this, such a surplus would push up the value of the pound.

3. A rising pound would make British exports more expensive abroad and imports cheaper.

4. British exports, and hence British manufacturing, which produced most of them, would decline as oil pushed up the value of the pound.

The solution to this being canvassed in the late 1970s was apparently simple: abolish exchange controls and let capital leave the UK. Old money going out would counterbalance the new money coming in from the North Sea. Thus there would be no balance of payments surplus and no rising pound. By 1977 this was the message coming from the financial journalists and the Conservative Party's spokesmen.[6]

In 1980 the economist Frank Blackaby quoted 'a senior Treasury official' as having said:

'Perhaps we can either have North Sea oil or manufacturing but not both.'[7]

So as British manufacturing shrank under Thatcher in the first Tory recession of 1979-82, the economics experts employed by the City were phlegmatic. Not to worry, they said, it is merely the mechanism through which the balance of trade between the UK and the rest of the world would correct itself. Importing less oil, we would need less manufacturing output. However, despite the abolition of exchange controls and a rush of capital out of the UK, the value of Sterling continued to rise between 1979 and 1981, destroying a quarter of the British manufacturing industry.

So why did this theory fail? The answer is that when the idea was being put about no one seems to have included in their speculations the possibility that the Government would also raise interest rates to control the money supply, as the monetarist Thatcher Government did. This made the pound doubly attractive to foreign investors and thus pushed its value higher, on top of the appreciation expected to arise from its status as a 'petrocurrency.'

'Freedom' for the financial sector also made a nonsense of the Thatcher Government's stated desire to control the money supply. As Lawson himself notes in his memoir (page 72), scrapping exchange controls meant that 'money aggregates [became] more difficult to predict and control.' With no exchange controls there was no control over money flowing in and out of the UK. For Lawson's 'more difficult' read 'impossible.' Not only could they not control the money supply, they couldn't even measure it.

The abolition of exchange controls and a Government willing to impose high interest rates 'to control the money supply' produced what Tom Nairn described as 'dream conditions for London's financial apparatus in 1980 and 1981.'[8] Accompanying this was the elaborate charade of 'self-regulation' - i.e. no regulation.

As the Thatcher recession deepened, British oil production and revenues to the Exchequer from it grew. But having become 'oil rich,' much of Britain, mired in recession, was getting poorer. Senior Treasury official at the time, Leo Pliatzky, wrote:

> 'It is understandable that people are frustrated that more primitive (sic) countries which produce oil have used the revenues from it to finance industrial and social development while in Britain *both have been cut back* since the North Sea oil came on stream.'[9] (Emphasis added.)

Economic policy and theory had *followed the money*. This isn't supposed to happen. Economic policy is supposed to be a rational business carried out by experts or 'social scientists.' But that is what happened: the theory followed the money. Frank Blackaby noted in 1980:

> 'Just at the time when oil output was building up, *there was a major swing in fashion in thinking about the exchange rate*. Up to 1977, the doctrine had been to use the exchange rate to preserve competitiveness [i.e. keep the pound relatively cheap]... The doctrine was then changed to assert that (a) there should be no exchange rate policy, and (b) that a high exchange rate was a good thing.' (Emphasis added.)

Blackaby called this:

> '...one of those *unfortunate accidents* which have so bedevilled British economic policy since the war.'[10] (Emphasis added.)

In the same year, *The Guardian*'s Victor Keegan asked:

> 'What happened to the oil revenues which, five years ago, led people to expect the dawning of a new age of prosperity? Most of it, in the *supreme irony of economic history*, has gone to pay

out unemployment to those who would not have lost their jobs if we had not discovered it in the first place.'[11] (Emphasis added.)

But hold on a minute. Are we supposed to believe that these changes in doctrine on the exchange rate which led to the recession of 1979-82 and the loss of two million jobs and the boom in the City of London, were the result of an 'ironic accident'? These 'changes in doctrine' occurred in 1977 when, after some months of debate in the economic press and the pages of *The Times*, 'the core institutional nexus,' i.e. the City, the Treasury and the Bank of England, plumped for oil rather than manufacturing and tried to persuade the Labour Government to do two things: allow the pound to rise and scrap exchange controls. Both were refused by the Callaghan Government. Both were introduced by Thatcher and Howe three years later.

The result was the 'loadsamoney' culture of the later 1980s, the shrinking manufacturing base accompanied by a booming City of London. Along the way the City's apologists changed the story. It wasn't that we had to lose manufacturing to make room for oil ('As the energy sector grows, something has to shrink.'[12]) but that Britain was on a natural evolutionary path towards becoming a post-manufacturing or post-industrial service economy. (Quite what that looked like, no one spelt out.) It did not matter that Britain was making fewer and fewer products because they would be replaced by 'financial products' (a term which came into use in the mid-1980s as the language followed the money). Former Treasury mandarin, Leo Pliatzky:

> 'It was a strange period to look back on. There appeared to be a great gulf between attitudes in much of the City and in industry throughout the country. In some quarters there was a Khomenei-like fanaticism about, a reluctance to see the connection between high interest rates and a crippling exchange rate. North Sea oil had made Sterling a petrocurrency, it was alleged; the days of manufacturing were over.'[13]

And what would happen when North Sea oil began to decline? Chancellor of the Exchequer Nigel Lawson believed, or pretended to believe, that as oil revenues declined, manufacturing, wrecked in the 1980s, would spontaneously regenerate itself![14]

Mrs Thatcher, who knew little about economics, bought the line (for a while) about the shift to a service economy. In his memoir, former BBC

44

political correspondent John Cole describes asking Mrs Thatcher for an example of how this 'service' or 'post-industrial economy' would work:

> 'She cited an entrepreneur she had met the previous week, who wished to take over Battersea power station and turn it into what we both then knew as a "Disneyland," but subsequently learned to call a theme park.'

The next day Cole recounted this to the Economic Attaché of the United States embassy:

> 'He looked at me in genuine astonishment, thoughtfully laid down his fork and exclaimed: "But gee, John, you can't all make a living opening doors for each other."'[15]

Nonetheless, these attitudes became the received wisdom within the Treasury. Political journalist Edward Pearce recounts how a 'Treasury knight,' i.e. one of the very senior civil servants in the Treasury, said to him of John Major's period in office:

> '...that though very fond of Mr Major, he worried a little at his anxiety about manufacturers. *He wasn't very happy with the analogies we made about Switzerland, so prosperous entirely from service industries*, so it was necessary to let him make friendly things (sic) to the manufacturing people.'[16] (Emphasis added.)

Fifteen years after they first appeared in financial circles, these attitudes were adopted by the New Thatcherites running the Labour Party. They talk of manufacturing being replaced, not by the 'service economy' but by the 'knowledge economy,' which is a vague mishmash of the City, computers, film production, rock music and the Internet. The difference these days is that, unlike John Major, New Labour hasn't even felt it necessary to 'make friendly things' to the 'manufacturing people' as they go down the drain. Here's Tony Blair addressing the Labour conference in September 1999 in typically verb-free sentences, on his vision of the world and 'the knowledge economy':

> 'Over a trillion dollars traded every day in currency markets and with them the fate of nations.
>
> Global finance and Communications and Media. Electronic commerce.

The Internet. The science of genetics. Every year a new revolution scattering in its wake security and ways of living for millions of people.

These forces of change driving the future:

Don't stop at national boundaries.

Don't respect tradition.

They wait for no one and no nation.

They are universal.

We know what a 21st-century nation needs.

A knowledge-based economy. A strong civic society. A confident place in the world.

Do that and a nation masters the future. Fail and it is the future's victim.

The challenge is how?

The answer is people.

The future is people.

The liberation of human potential not just as workers but as citizens.

Not power to the people but power to each person to make the most of what is within them.

People are born with talent and everywhere it is in chains.'

There was a supplement about 'the knowledge economy' in the *The New Statesman*, 27 September 1999. Near the end of this a number of well-known names are asked about the knowledge 'the world needs now.' James Dyson, the inventor and manufacturer of the 'Cyclone' vacuum cleaner, dumped a bucket of cold water on 'the knowledge economy' idea:

'What I think we're losing is our intellectual property base, our know-how in both technology and manufacturing. We're losing the ability to make planes, cars, electrical appliances, in almost every traditional manufacturing area. That's a terrible thing. While you might think the world now depends on the software and service industries, in reality their output is a fraction of the traditional industries. I've had an argument with the governor of the Bank of England about this, *who thinks that software is replacing the need to make goods*.' (Emphasis added.)

In the late 1970s and 1980s the bankers first thought it was oil which would replace manufacturing. Then it was the growth of the City of London and the financial services sector. Now the Governor of the Bank of England thinks it is computer software.

In his comment Dyson concluded:

> 'If nothing is done about our dwindling technical know-how, we will end up as a very weak service economy. We'll have no manufacturing, few jobs and end up a very poor country. Tony Blair and Gordon Brown realise this...'

Do they? I wonder. And is it not striking that in the past few years the single biggest British economic success story has been the Dyson vacuum cleaner - old-fashioned manufacturing - and not the much vaunted dot.com companies, most of which have gobbled up a lot of start-up money, enriched their founders and gone bust. [17]

Intellectually, historically, geographically and institutionally the Labour Party was the party of manufacturing (the 'real economy') and the response of its leaders in the early 1980s was to resist all this drift away from manufacturing. How could they not? The party's constituencies were being hammered. The idea that there was a basic conflict between the City (which benefited the South) and industry was well established in the party in the early 1980s. It wasn't a hard sell. The City was booming but the industrial North, Scotland and Wales were deep in a recession induced by the high interest rates and high pound policy.

Neil Kinnock, who replaced Michael Foot as leader of the Labour Party after the election loss in 1983, was influenced by a version of the City-versus-industry thesis by the economist John Eatwell. In the middle of the first Thatcher recession of the early 1980s Eatwell had written a TV series *Whatever Happened To Britain?* (and later a book of the series) which argued that the recovery of the British economy centred on the reconstruction of manufacturing, and that this entailed the adoption of something like the German or French relationship between manufacturing and finance capital, i.e. ending the City's dominance of British economic policy.[18] These views were reflected in Neil Kinnock's 1986 book *Making*

Our Way. They were certainly the views of the then-important Shadow Cabinet figure Bryan Gould, and are even to be found in Gordon Brown's 1989 book *Where There Is Greed*. Thus, as far as their published statements are concerned, in 1987 there was something like a consensus on economic policy at the top of the Labour Party, i.e. the problem was the dominance of the City. Economic policies which benefited the City - high interest rates, the overvalued pound and no exchange controls - damaged manufacturing.

With the exception of Bryan Gould, the leadership of the Labour Party abandoned all this between 1988 and 1989. Precisely when is not in the public record. Labour Party documents rather than books written by its leaders show that by 1986 the Labour leadership had begun accommodating the perceived power, and electoral popularity, of a Thatcherised, privatising Britain. Central to that change was abandoning the belief that the Government should, or could, take action to control the financial sector in the interests of the rest of the economy.[19] Nor is it possible to be precise about why this happened because the participants have not given us enough detail. However, a number of factors played a part. One factor was membership of the then European Economic Community (EEC). After the 1983 election defeat, Labour's attitude to the EEC was uncertain. The party, and the Parliamentary Party, was divided. After the 1975 Referendum on EEC membership which produced a 'yes' vote, the leadership had accepted the verdict of the electorate but by 1983, with the rise of the Bennite left, the party had become 'anti-EEC' again.

After the 1983 defeat, opinion in the Labour Party began to shift. The Labour left's policies (including withdrawal from the EEC), as expressed in the 'longest suicide note in history,' had been so heavily defeated in the 1983 election that their views were discredited. The party began to have success in European Parliamentary elections, and EEC money began to arrive in Britain for infrastructure projects. This began to influence Labour local authorities which were receiving nothing but cuts and attacks from the Tory central Government in London. This shift was reflected inside the trade unions and, by the end of 1984, while the TUC's General Congress remained against British membership, its full-time officials, the TUC Secretariat, were 'following a de facto pro-European policy.'[20] Under constant assault from the Government, trade union officials began to perceive that their future might be brighter in the EEC where unions were seen to be legitimate players.

The financial deregulation of the 1980s and the creation of the global casino economy via the computer chip, created a climate in which it became a commonplace to believe that the nation state, and thus national economic policies, were less and less viable. This line was exploited by the pro-Europe lobby to influence the growing 'green' awareness in the 1980s. Arguments such as 'pollution is a European problem and needs European solutions' became common.[21]

This attitude was massively reinforced when Mrs Thatcher began to be perceived as a 'little Englander' and anti-Europe. Thatcher's support for the anti-EEC position contaminated it in the eyes of many in the Labour Party.[22] (If Maggie was against it, it couldn't be all bad.) Finally, although it is not quite true that the Labour leadership under Neil Kinnock became pro-EEC *because* opinion polls showed the EEC to be popular at the time, by the third election defeat in 1987, had opinion polls shown the EEC to be unpopular, Labour would not have supported membership. After the 1987 election defeat, the Kinnock-led Parliamentary Party was not prepared to challenge public opinion in *any* major area.

Meanwhile...

At the 1983 election Tony Blair and Gordon Brown won safe Labour seats in the Labour heartlands of North East England and Scotland respectively. Brown was already a substantial figure in the Scottish Labour Party. Blair, on the other hand, was an unknown. But by the end of their first parliament in 1987 both had been noticed as rising stars and had been given shadow cabinet roles. Brown was understudy to the late John Smith, who was shadowing the Department of Trade and Industry. It was, Brown's biographer Paul Routledge commented, 'the fastest rise through the Opposition ranks since the 1950s.'[23]

The US Government was also paying attention. In 1986, after three years in Parliament, Tony Blair took the 'freebie' tour of the States. At the end of the trip, although still formally a member of the Campaign for Nuclear Disarmament, Blair announced to a dinner party in Washington that the visit had persuaded him of the value of nuclear weapons.[24]

Notes

1. These measures are proudly listed by Nigel Lawson in his memoir, *The View From No.11* (London: Corgi, 1992) on page 626.

2. Lawson (see note 1), page 39.

3. On page 41 of his memoir (see note 1), Lawson tells us that without the abolition of exchange controls, 'the City would have been hard put to remain a world-class financial centre.' What, no reference to the interests of the wider economy, Nigel? We are astounded (not).

4. Margaret Thatcher, *The Downing Street Years* (London: HarperCollins, 1993), page 44. Lawson '...had no doubt that, with Sterling buoyed up by the combination of its petrocurrency status and growing international confidence in the sound monetary policies of the new Government - whatever they might turn out to be! - early and complete abolition was not only achievable but economically necessary.' Lawson (see note 1), page 39.

5. *The Observer*, 2 May 1999.

6. In a speech in July 1977, Shadow Chancellor Geoffrey Howe claimed that scrapping exchange controls would *prevent* the pound rising too far and damaging manufacturing. On 27 August 1977, *The Times* reported Shadow Cabinet member Leon Brittan stating that, 'the best use the UK could make of the economic benefits of North Sea oil would be to let the pound rise in a genuinely free float.' On 29 October 1977, it reported Shadow Treasury minister David Howell advocating a 'strong pound.' On 1 November 1977, it reported Shadow Chancellor Geoffrey Howe claiming that 'Relaxation [of exchange controls] would also prevent the pound from rising artificially high and damaging the competitiveness of our exports...' The general tenor of the oil debate can be seen at a glance in *The Times* Index for 1977, especially page 375, under Economic Situation and Policy.

For the most influential financial journalist of the period, Samuel Brittan, scrapping exchange controls was the 'only serious way of preventing North Sea oil from imposing a contraction in manufacturing...' *The Financial Times,* 3 July 1980. Brittan's piece was headed, 'Deindustrialisation Is Good For The UK.' The same view was expressed by Roy Peters in 'Overseas Portfolio Investment - Developments Since The Abolition Of Exchange Controls,' *NatWest Quarterly Review*, May 1981: 'It may be that the only way to protect manufacturing industry in the short term is to ensure that there are sufficient outflows on the capital account to stop Sterling rising further.'

There are, of course, other ways to prevent a currency appreciating, of which maintaining low interest rates is the most frequently used. Japan and West Germany followed this course for decades. But low interest rates don't benefit the City...

7. Frank Blackaby, 'Exchange Rate Policy And Economic Strategy,' *Three Banks Review*, June 1980.

8. Tom Nairn, *The Break-Up Of Britain* (London: Verso, 1981), page 392.

9. Leo Pliatzky, *The Treasury Under Mrs Thatcher* (Oxford: Basil Blackwell, 1989), page 194.

10. Blackaby (see note 7).

11. Victor Keegan, *The Guardian*, 16 May 1983.

12. Hamish MacRae, *The Guardian*, 13 October 1981. In this curious universe it is unclear how countries ever get richer, for as one sector grows, another, apparently, has to shrink. Did the Saudis have to grow fewer dates after they became oil producers?

13. Pliatzky (see note 9), page 128.

14. Nigel Lawson (see note 1), pages 195/6. Not so far, Nigel.

15. John Cole, *As It Seemed To Me* (London: Weidenfeld and Nicolson, 1995), page 209.

16. *The Guardian*, 8 January 1992.

17. I owe this observation to my editor, Paul Duncan.

18. John Eatwell, *Whatever Happened To Britain?* (London: Duckworth/BBC, 1982). This is a view not dissimilar to that expressed by Edward Heath in the early 1970s.

19. Neil Kinnock, *Making Our Way* (Oxford: Blackwell, 1986). See Eric Shaw, *The Labour Party Since 1979* (London: Routledge, 1994), pages 46-50, for a concise account of the policy shifts in this period.

20. Paul Teague, 'The TUC And The European Community,' *Millennium: Journal Of International Studies*, Vol. 18, No.1, page 36.

21. Further, the experience of the French Government in 1982/3 seemed to confirm the futility of action by individual states. This is discussed in chapter 7.

22. Labour's shifting EEC policies are surveyed by Andrew Geddes, 'Labour And The European Community 1973-93,' *Contemporary Record*, Vol. 8, No.2, Autumn 1994.

23. Paul Routledge, *Gordon Brown: The Biography* (London: Simon and Schuster, 1998), page 141.

24. Michael Elliott, 'Lessons From An American Journey,' *The Observer*, 14 April 1996.

5. From The Welsh Windbag To Bambi

The big changes in the Labour Party's policies began after the election defeat in 1987. After 'a covert operation by the Solidarity network to ensure advancement for John Smith,'[1] Smith became Shadow Chancellor, with Gordon Brown his deputy as the Shadow Chief Secretary to the Treasury. Smith was a very traditional Labour Party figure, an economics spokesperson who knew little about economics. An Economic Secretariat was created around Smith.[2] This group was made up of:

> '...full-time advisers *with degrees in economics*... supplemented by a network of high-powered economists, several of whom had previously believed that Britain should go it alone in a drive to expand the economy and reduce unemployment, *but had now been won over to the stability and shelter of the European monetary system*.'[3] (Emphases added.)

The 'high-powered economists' came from the City of London: Gavyn Davies from Goldman Sachs; Neil Mackinnon from Yamaichi; and Gerald Holtham from Shearson Lehman Hutton. Davies is the interesting one. He had been an economic advisor to the Callaghan Government of 1976-9 and has been one of the Blair Government's main financial advisors.

By 1988 Labour leader Neil Kinnock, John Smith and Gordon Brown (and their advisers) had concluded that Labour should embrace UK membership of the then EEC and that it should advocate British membership of the European Exchange Rate Mechanism (ERM) as the first step towards an eventual single European currency.[4] Kinnock had come round to support British membership of the EEC having been against it earlier in his career. Smith had always been in favour. But the Labour leadership did not decide to advocate ERM membership for economic reasons but because it was perceived by them to be a way of demonstrating to the City that they were trustworthy. ERM membership would be a guarantee there would be no more attempts to run an independent economic policy. By 1988 most of Labour's leaders had concluded that the City of London was too powerful to challenge. *This is the origin of New Labour*. Smith was quoted in *The Sunday Times*: 'Labour policy was quick to be ahead of the game with ERM entry *which the City liked*.'[5] (Emphasis added.)

Gordon Brown and John Smith seem to have had a very rosy view of the ERM. In 1971 banker and Conservative MP Edward du Cann was present when Conservative MPs were briefed on the Competition and

Credit Control proposals (the first (and disastrous) attempt to 'free' the British banks, discussed in chapter 1) and saw that hardly anybody in the room had the faintest idea what was being discussed. Seventeen years later, Labour MP and then senior member of the Shadow Cabinet, Bryan Gould had a similar experience:

> 'I remember [Gordon] Brown addressing the Parliamentary Labour Party on the great advantages of joining the ERM, using arguments I knew to be erroneous. He suggested that by fixing the parity within the ERM, we would be applying socialist planning to the economy, rather than leaving an important issue to market forces. *The party responded warmly to the notion that speculators would be disarmed.* They all seemed unaware that the only thing which gave speculators their chance was a Government foolish enough to defend a parity seen to be out of line with a currency's real value... John Smith and Gordon Brown *truly believed* that the ERM was a new, magical device which would insulate their decisions about the currency against reality.'[6] (Emphases added.)

By this time Gould was being discarded by the leadership group around Kinnock. His swansong was the May 1989 policy document *Meet The Challenge, Make The Change*. Gould had chaired the working party which put together the section on economic policy and the document contained much of his thinking. At the centre of it was the structural conflict between the interests of the financial sector (the City, the bankers) and the manufacturing economy. *Meet The Challenge, Make The Change* was the policy expression of the previous five year's experience of the British domestic economy being hammered by the City of London.[7]

Gould was going to be dumped at some point, and his hostility to the UK joining the Exchange Rate Mechanism provided the reason. He was moved out of Labour's economics team when the pro-ERM decision was taken. This policy shift led to Gould's eventual resignation from the Labour Party and Parliament. He was the only Labour MP to pay a significant price for Labour's great policy shift towards the market, Europe and NATO after the 1987 defeat.

On the basis that the ERM would defeat speculators and provide a stable environment for economic growth, John Smith won support for joining the ERM at the Labour conference in 1989. On 16 November, at a meeting of the Shadow Cabinet, the new Labour economic orthodoxy was spelt out:

'The idea that the state could stimulate the economy, either by expanding the nationalised industries or through local councils, was out, [Shadow Chancellor] Smith told them. The Government was not going to raise enough through taxes or borrowing because, other considerations aside, *the rules of the ERM prevented it*. This would mean... meeting industrial and financial leaders to establish trust before election day. "We can leave dogmatism to the Tories," he said. So began the 'prawn cocktail offensive...''[8] (Emphasis added.)

'...*the rules of the ERM prevented it*...' Here was the reason for the enthusiasm of the inner group for the ERM. It was a final straightjacket. By wearing it, a Labour Government could not pursue growth and employment through public spending and increased taxation. The City would be reassured and it would play with the electorate. Labour's pollsters were telling them that to get elected they had to be more convincing on economic policy, especially on an anti-inflation policy because the electorate still blamed them for the inflation in the 1970s and ensuing industrial strife. Despite the Tory inflation of the 1970s, followed by the Tory recession of the early 1980s *and* the renewed inflation of the late 1980s, people still perceived the Tories to be more competent with the economy than Labour. This is the power of the myth but also a sad indictment of the sheer political incompetence of the Labour Party leadership. It is also a tribute to the control of the economic agenda being wielded by the City, via the Conservative Party, in the 1980s because they had convinced people that their interests and economic 'common sense' were identical. There was an alternative, Bryan Gould's option, which was to challenge the intellectual hegemony of the City. This was rejected. Kinnock, Smith and Brown chose surrender. Or, they would say, realism.

The City liked the ERM because it knew that, as the ERM had been sold to British politicians of both parties as an anti-inflation device, this ensured that the pound would enter the ERM at a high Sterling/Deutschmark value, requiring high interest rates to sustain it. It was the high interest rates which guaranteed that the ERM would, as they used to say, 'bear down on inflation.' (Entry at too high a Sterling/Deutschmark exchange rate is what happened when the Tories took the UK into the ERM in 1990.) Keeping interest rates high would produce a depressed domestic economy. And so, voila!, the ERM would deliver low inflation on the one hand and, on the other hand (where the real agenda was coming from), good times for the City of London as high interest rates attracted the world's speculative money and domestic loans paid off handsomely.

Lunching For Labour

The 'prawn cocktail offensive,' referred to by McSmith in the last quotation above, saw members of the Shadow Cabinet, chiefly John Smith and Marjorie Mowlam, touring the dining rooms of the City of London, assuring their hosts that, despite the City's role in the assault on the British domestic economy in the previous decade and some of the biggest rip-offs in British history, Labour had no intention of making their lives any less profitable than they had been under Mrs Thatcher. John Smith's 'establishing trust' with business and financial leaders turned out to mean, 'Trust us, we will do nothing of which you do not approve.' At one such meeting:

> 'International currency dealers were promised there would be no attempt to bring back exchange controls. That genie is out of the bottle, Smith declared.'[9]

At another meeting, Smith received an ovation from an audience of bankers for announcing that Labour did not intend to nationalise the banks - something which the party had not seriously considered in the previous fifty years![10]

The 'prawn cocktail offensive' was the most complete and protracted act of political surrender in 20th-century British history. It marked the end of the post-war Labour Party. Although it played well in the City, there were some reservations there. Was the change real? And despite what its creators tell us was a brilliant election campaign, it didn't quite work with the electorate and Labour narrowly lost the 1992 election - the fourth successive defeat. Neil Kinnock quit and John Smith became Labour leader, defeating Bryan Gould.[11]

John Smith And Bilderberg

In political circles the late John Smith is remembered with great reverence, one of the great 'lost leaders' of British politics.[12] What this is based on escapes me. The Labour left says things like, 'Well, he was an honest right-winger.' *And that's all?* Much of this now appears to me to be nothing more than code for Smith's dislike of Peter Mandelson.[13] There are other dimensions to Smith's political career which are not referred to by his biographer Andy McSmith and of which virtually all Labour Party members are unaware. From 1989 to 1992 Smith was a member of the Steering Committee, the inner circle, of the Bilderberg Group,[14] one of the leading forums promoting the transnational, American-dominated interests which are now gobbling up the world. There is nothing in the official record of John Smith's life which even hints at such a role, of him having that kind of status. As far as we know, and public records are incomplete, from the recent disclosures of attendees at Bilderberg meetings, Smith had not even been invited to a meeting before joining the Steering Committee. Did the steering group invitation arise from his many meetings with the bankers of London, some of whom would have been to Bilderberg meetings? Or did his parade round the City of London in 1989 announcing Labour's conversion to his hosts' way of thinking come after Bilderberg?

What was it about Smith that Bilderberg personnel thought qualified him for such a role? Was it simply the Bilderberg people seeing a good opportunity to co-opt a future British prime minister and, in the process, help neutralise a potentially troublesome political party? When Smith joined the Steering Committee Mrs Thatcher was refusing to allow the UK to join the Exchange Rate Mechanism and was thus holding up the European unification movement.[15] It was a reasonable calculation in 1989 that Mrs Thatcher, who was becoming increasingly unpopular, would not go on forever and that the next British prime minister would be from the Labour Party. After Kinnock, Smith was next in line.

While Smith was on the steering group of Bilderberg, Gordon Brown attended one of its meetings with him in 1991. This was Labour's shadow chancellor and his deputy meeting the international movers and shakers of transnational finance. It was an education for and validation of Gordon Brown from the top table of capital. More 'trust' being established... This was the same year as the publication of Brown's radical critique of the Thatcher years, *Where There Is Greed*.[16]

Then there is Smith's friendship with Baroness (Meta) Ramsay, the career MI6 officer, whose friendship with Smith began at university. She became President of the Scottish Union of Students and went on to work in the murky world of Cold War international student politics. *Private Eye* 973 of 2 April 1999 noted that Jack Straw, while an official of the National Union of Students, visited Chile in 1966. His trip was sponsored by the Foundation for International Student Co-operation, an MI6 front whose manager at the time was Ramsay.[17] Now retired from 'the diplomatic service,' Baroness Ramsay was a member of the Executive of the Labour Finance and Industry Group (LFIG) and in edition 5 of the *LFIG News* (1997) she was described as Foreign Policy Adviser to John Smith (1992-4). In 1997 she became Chair of the Atlantic Council and she has since been appointed to the Parliamentary Intelligence and Security Committee.[18]

The MI6 theme in Smith's career extends a little further. John Smith's widow, Lady Smith, is on the board of an MI6 front organisation.

> 'Baroness Smith has recently been appointed a director of the Hakluyt Foundation... established in 1995 by the late Sir Fitzroy Maclean... managing director, Christopher James... Baroness Smith joins Sir Brian Cubbon, a former top civil servant, Lord Laing of Dunphail, Treasurer of the Conservative Party towards the end of the Thatcher period... Earl Jellicoe... Sir Peter Cazalet, director of the P and O Group, former BP Chairman... and Sir Peter Holmes, one-time managing director of Shell... [Hakluyt's] brochure makes clear that clients can expect information they "will not receive by the usual Government and commercial routes."'[19]

Smith gets money from a group of 'sympathetic businessmen'... and gets invited into the inner circle of one of the world's most secretive and, perhaps, most influential corporate forums... and his widow joins the board of a trust which manages an MI6 front... It isn't clear to me what these fragments add up to and without more information (which we are unlikely to get, given the way the UK works) we will probably never know. Was John Smith an asset of MI6? Possibly. It would be an unusual MI6 officer (Meta Ramsay) who didn't use her friendship with a rising Labour politician. Was John Smith, like Tony Blair, merely an admirer of the managers of the corporate world, for whom, after all, agencies like MI6 are working? Possibly. But would admiration be enough to get you into the Bilderberg Steering Committee? Without more information we cannot draw a conclusion beyond this: whatever Smith was he was a good deal more complicated than the public image of the genial, whiskey-drinking, Scots lawyer who liked walking the mountains.

Whatever he was and whoever his sponsors were in the corporate world, it was Smith as Shadow Chancellor, along with party leader Neil Kinnock, who discarded the philosophy underlying Labour's economic policies for the previous 40 years. Neil Kinnock's economic adviser at the time John Eatwell, summed up their new philosophy in 1992.

> '1. Abandonment of the idea that short-term macroeconomics management is the key to the maintenance of full employment. It is argued that it is no longer possible to have Keynesianism in one country, and hence fine-tuning should be replaced by a

search for macroeconomic stability as a framework for long-term investment...

2. Replacement of hostility towards the European Commission, in which the EC was seem as an inhibition upon Labour's policies, with an enthusiasm for the EC as an arena within which Labour's objectives can be best attained...

3. Abandonment of the idea that nationalisation of an industry is necessarily the best way to achieve efficiency, and its replacement by the proposition that regulation may achieve the same results.

4. Replacement of the idea that industrial policy should involve the Government in making tactical management decision with the proposition that the state should provide the 'well-springs' of growth - skills, research and development, infrastructure - within a broad strategy of accumulation...'[20]

This was a rejection of the Bryan Gould committee's policies of only 3 years earlier, a rejection of the thinking underlying Neil Kinnock's book *Making Our Way* and Gordon Brown's *Where There Is Greed,* and post-war Labour economic thinking. The Thatcher revolution, the imposition of neo-liberal, free market thinking on the UK was thus virtually complete. There would be no further Labour opposition to the American-dominated global casino economy.

Neil Lawson, former aid to Gordon Brown, said of this period:

'Labour got to the stage in the early 1990s where we'd give up virtually anything to get elected.'[21]

By 1992 they *had* given up virtually everything.

Going Down For The Fourth Time

Despite vigorous waving of the white flag of surrender, in 1992 the Labour Party lost its fourth election in a row. However, in America Bill Clinton led the Democrats to a surprise victory ending 12 years (8 of Reagan, 4 of Bush) of Republican control of the White House. Mrs Thatcher's relationship with Ronald Reagan, and her position as an idol of both American and British Conservatives, had pulled the Conservative and Republican Parties much closer in the 1980s than was usually the case. During the American election of 1992, a group of Republican Party staffers visited Conservative Party HQ and copied some of the Major election campaign's themes and techniques. The Major Government even obliged the Republicans by asking, on their behalf, the British secret services if there was any dirt on Bill Clinton from his stay as a Rhodes Scholar at Oxford.[22] On the other wing, a number of Labour Party personnel and allies, including focus group and advertising man Philip Gould, worked on the Democratic campaign in minor capacities and they brought back knowledge of the Democratic election and media operations.

After the 1992 American Presidential election, Brown and Blair went out to America to meet the new Democratic Government. In Washington, Brown and Blair met Clinton's people. These meetings were arranged by Jonathan Powell, Political Secretary at the US Embassy. (Powell apparently quit his diplomatic career and joined Tony Blair as chief of staff in 1995.[23]) They also met: Larry Summers, a Harvard academic who went on to join the World Bank; Robert Reich, Clinton's newly-appointed Labour Secretary; and Alan Greenspan, chair of the Federal Reserve, roughly equivalent to the governor of the Bank of England. These latter meetings were arranged by a young *Financial Times* journalist called Ed Balls, who had studied under Summers at Harvard. (Balls later joined Gordon Brown as his economic advisor.) Like other Labour personnel, including Yvette Cooper MP, whom Balls later married, and David Miliband, head of Blair's policy unit, Balls had spent a year in America as a Kennedy Scholar.[24] In London a series of meetings were held between Democratic Party staffers and their Labour equivalents.[25]

Self-styled modernisers Blair and Brown had a problem because the incumbent leader of the Labour Party, John Smith, would not go down the 'modernising' route fast enough for them. Reading between the lines, Smith knew that all he had to do was wait for the Tories to lose the next election. To go down the Brown/Blair route would mean major aggravation with the Labour Party members and unions, and why bother? Smith's very sympathetic biographer, Andy McSmith, titles the final chapter of his biography 'Masterly Inactivity' but *any* kind of inactivity was not what Blair and Brown had in mind. Brown began to regret that he hadn't challenged John Smith for the leadership of the party. The inevitable tactical conflict that was brewing was obviated by Smith's death from a heart attack in 1994.[26]

Notes

1. Andy McSmith, *John Smith: A Life 1938-94* (London: Mandarin, 1994), page 154. What this 'covert operation' actually amounted to, McSmith doesn't say. Solidarity was the most important centre/right faction within the Parliamentary Labour Party of the time. It had been formed in 1981 to meet the challenge from the Bennite left. See McSmith, page 115.

2. This is probably but not certainly the Political Economy Unit funded to the tune of £200,000 by the Labour MP Geoffrey Robinson. See Tom Bower, *The Paymaster: Geoffrey Robinson, Maxwell And New Labour* (London: Simon and Schuster, 2001), page 89. Earlier in his career, Smith's biographer tells us, 'a group of sympathetic industrialists had been so impressed by Smith that they had clubbed together to provide money for an extra researcher.' McSmith (see note 1), page 142. 'A group of sympathetic industrialists,' but McSmith gives us no names. My *guess* would be that Smith was being funded by British United Industrialists (BUI), an organisation which existed solely to funnel business money into British politics, mostly to anti-left and anti-union groups. For example BUI helped to fund the working miners during the miners' strike of the 1980s.

3. McSmith (see note 1), page 157. That McSmith thought it worth mentioning that some of John Smith's advisors had degrees in economics speaks volumes for the economic illiteracy taken for granted among the Parliamentary Labour Party. You might think that understanding the British economy would be... well, kind of important to a Labour MP. Not so. Economics is regarded as a specialist subject, akin to, say, Albanian politics, best left to experts. Indeed, understanding economics can be damaging to the careers of Labour MPs as it can lead them to question the wisdom of the policies being handed down by the leadership. Bryan Gould is the best recent example of this.

4. ERM policy was decided by Neil Kinnock, Smith, Gordon Brown and John Eatwell, Kinnock's economic advisor. McSmith (see note 1), page 192.

5. 1 March 1992.

6. *The Guardian*, 19 August 1995.

7. In my view this is still the correct analysis. Was there really a chance that Labour would adopt and proselytise policies attacking the City of London? In retrospect the answer is 'no.' Adopting an anti-City policy would have guaranteed the Labour Party even more hostility from the

media than they had been receiving for their anti-nuclear policy of the 1980s. The City in the mid-1980s had achieved almost total dominance of opinion formation on matters of the economy. I know what an anti-City campaign would look like (who doesn't hate the bankers?) but the difficulties would have been formidable. Recognition of the existence of a structural conflict within British society is the big no-no and Labour's leaders tiptoed up to it, had a look and decided 'No can do.' While Brown and Kinnock may have recognised the City/industry conflict in books, both had privately been shifting away from this position for the previous two or three years, towards greater accommodation with the City.

It is worth noting here, as an interesting insight into the nature of political life, that while Gould was beavering away (and he and the committee took this very seriously, called dozens of opinions) his party leader and two other senior colleagues knew they were going to ditch what he and the committee had produced before the report had been written.

8. McSmith (see note 1), page 209.

9. McSmith (see note 1), page 210.

10. McSmith (see note 1), page 210.

11. Labour got more votes in 1992 and lost, than Labour did in 2001 when it won a landslide.

12. See, for example: Peter Dobie, 'For John's Sake, End Your Silence Now, Elizabeth,' *The Mail On Sunday*, 28 March 1999; Ken Livingston, 'John Smith Made Mistakes But At Least He Was Trusted,' *The Independent*, 12 May 1999; and the eulogistic foreword to the paperback edition of Andy McSmith's biography, *John Smith*. Even left-wing former MEP Ken Coates offers a version of this in his review of a collection of John Smith's speeches in *The Spokesman*, No.71.

Part of the shock apparently felt by the British political establishment was the loss not of the leader of the Labour Party (would they have long mourned Neil Kinnock?) but of the next prime minister. When he died in 1994, everyone in the Westminster game, not least Smith himself, knew that Labour would win the next election. Or, more accurately, everyone knew that the Tories would lose.

13. Peter Oborne, *Alastair Campbell: New Labour And The Rise Of The Media Class* (London: Aurum Press, 1999), page 96: 'John Smith promptly thrust him [Mandelson] into the outer darkness.'

14. Letter from Maja Banck, Executive Secretary of Bilderberg Meetings, to the author, 13 April 1999: 'the late John Smith has been a member of our Steering Committee between 1989 and 1992.' Presumably he left

after becoming leader of the Labour Party in 1992. The best Website on Bilderberg is www.bilderberg.org/

15. See Chancellor Nigel Lawson's comments in his memoir, *The View From No.11* (London: Corgi, 1992), pages 898/9. The now defunct far-right group, Western Goals Institute, tried, without any evidence, to trace all Mrs Thatcher's post-1989 difficulties to the 1989 Bilderberg meeting in a 'Viewpoint Paper,' *Hit-Job On Margaret Thatcher* of April 1990.

16. Edinburgh: Mainstream, 1989. In this book Brown was still articulating a version of the City-versus-industry thesis, though with few hostages to fortune by way of policies. Given the gap between writing books and getting them published, this might have been finished anything up to a year before it appeared. Its existence is a measure of the complete switch in thinking among the Labour leaders which occurred in the summer of 1989. Curiously enough, this book is not referred to in the Routledge biography of Brown. Neither is the visit to Bilderberg.

17. This story appeared first in *The Mail On Sunday*, 28 March 1999.

18. The text of speech by Defence Secretary George Robertson, 'NATO For A New Generation,' given to the National Conference of the Atlantic Council, 19 November 1997, begins with Robertson congratulating Ramsay on becoming Chair.

19. David Osler, 'Privileged Information,' *Red Pepper*, January 1999, page 35.

The Hakluyt Foundation is a trust and it directs the activities of Hakluyt and Co. Ltd. The Hakluyt Foundation was first identified in 'Top Firms Get Secrets From MI6' by Mark Watts in *Sunday Business*, 11 October 1998. '*Sunday Business* has identified an MI6 cut-out organisation, The Hakluyt Foundation, which channels intelligence from the agency to big companies and gathers information from its own contacts. It is run by Richard Tomlinson's old MI6 boss, Christopher James, who retired from the agency in 1994. Other directors include a former Royal Dutch Shell managing director and a one-time Home Office permanent secretary.' The publication of this story earned *Sunday Business* a visit from an MI6 official. See also Nicholas Rufford, 'Cloak And Dagger,' *Management Today*, February 1999, which named another MI6 officer, Mike Reynolds, as one of the co-founders of Hakluyt with Christopher James. On Hakluyt see also Mark Hollingsworth, 'An Equitable Life For Some,' *Punch* 136, August 2001.

On Hakluyt and another apparent MI6 front, Ciex, see also 'Spies Defect From MI6 To Shadowy Careers In The City,' *The Sunday Times*, 15 November 1998. According to ex-MI6 officer Richard Tomlinson,

Ciex is a pun on C/X, the in-house term used by MI6 for secret intelligence.

In June 2001 Hakluyt was revealed to have employed a German filmmaker to spy on Greenpeace and other environmental groups. See Maurice Chittenden and Nicholas Rufford, 'MI6 "Firm" Spied On Green Groups,' *The Sunday Times*, 17 June 2001.

20. Reproduced here from Paul Anderson and Nyta Mann, *Safety First: The Making Of New Labour* (London: Granta Books, 1997), pages 72/3.

21. Quoted in Francis Wheen's column in *The Guardian*, 7 February 2001. Lawson was a founder member of the lobbying company Lawson Lucas Mendlesohn.

22. The only 'dirt' from that period on Clinton is the allegation, from an anonymous former CIA officer, that Clinton was recruited by the CIA to keep tabs on fellow Americans at Oxford in the Agency's monitoring of opponents of the Vietnam War.

23. I use 'apparently' here because it is possible that he was simply seconded from the Foreign and Commonwealth Office to the Blair office.

24. This is a British-funded scheme which sends young Brits across the Atlantic to see how things should be done, keep the Anglo-American alliance going, blah blah. There is an account of the Kennedy scholarship system by the current chair of the committee which picks them, Peter Hennessy, in the education supplement to *The Independent*, 1 May 1997.

25. For some details see Paul Routledge, *Gordon Brown: The Biography* (London: Simon and Schuster, 1998), pages 175/6.

26. On that conflict and the modernisers' impatience with Smith see Jon Sopel, *Tony Blair: The Moderniser* (London: Michael Joseph, 1995), chapter 7, and Phillip Gould, *The Unfinished Revolution* (London: Little,Brown, 1998), pages 191/2. There has been the occasional suggestion that perhaps Smith was poisoned to make way for 'the modernisers,' a rather thrilling idea for which there is, sadly, not a shred of evidence.

6. New Friends - The Israeli Connection

In January 1994, three months before John Smith's death, the then shadow Home Secretary Tony Blair, with wife Cherie Booth, went on a trip to Israel at the Israeli Government's expense. Incidentally, this trip is not mentioned in either the Sopel nor Rentoul biographies of Blair.[1] Blair had always been sympathetic to Israel, had shared chambers with Board of Deputies of British Jews President Eldred Tabachnik,[2] and had joined the Labour Friends of Israel on becoming an MP.

Two months after returning from Israel, Tony Blair was introduced to Michael Levy at a dinner party by Gideon Meir, the number two in the Israeli embassy in London. Levy was a retired businessman who had made his money creating and then selling a successful record company, and had become a major fund-raiser for Jewish charities. Levy was 'dazzled by Blair's drive and religious commitment' and the two men became friends.[3]

A month later the leader of the Labour Party, John Smith, died, and Blair won the leadership election contest with Gordon Brown. In some accounts, he had financial assistance from Levy.[4] All accounts are agreed that Michael Levy then set about raising money (the figure of £7 million is widely quoted) for the personal use of his new 'friend,' Tony Blair, leader of the Labour Party. The big early contributors to the 'blind trust' which funded Blair's office were:

> '...a group of businessmen involved in Jewish charities whose decisions to give to Labour have been crucially influenced by the party's strong pro-Israeli stance under both Tony Blair and his predecessor John Smith... Levy brought the world of North London Jewish business into the Labour Party... some of the names whom Levy persuaded to donate include Sir Emmanuel Kaye of Kaye Enterprises, Sir Trevor Chinn of Lex Garages, Maurice Hatter of IMO Precision Control and David Goldman of the Sage software group... it is clear, however, that for this group Blair's (and Smith's before him) strong support for Israel is an important factor, especially with those such as Kaye, Chinn and Levy himself, who raise large sums for Israeli causes. Nick Cosgrave, director of Labour Friends of Israel, says Blair "brought back Labour Friends of Israel into the Labour Party, in a sense... before the majority of supporters of Labour Friends felt uncomfortable with the Labour Party.'[5]

Back in 1994 it was clear that, barring a miracle, the Tories would lose the next General Election. Tony Blair was widely recognised as one of Labour's coming men; and there had already been speculation in the media (notably in *The Sunday Times*) that he would succeed John Smith as Labour leader. It is hard to read this account of the events from Blair's trip to Israel to the funding of his private office and *not* conclude that the Israeli Government had spotted Blair as a very pro-Israeli politician and possible leader of the Labour Party and steered him towards the leading Jewish fund-raiser in London.

As leader of the party, with the Levy-raised money in his 'blind trust,' Blair achieved financial independence from the trade unions and the Labour Party. Blair hated the Labour Party and viewed it as his enemy.[6] With the Levy money Blair was able to begin expanding his private office and he hired Alastair Campbell, former Political Editor at *The Daily Mirror*, as his press officer in September 1994 and diplomat Jonathan Powell as his chief of staff in January 1995. The Labour Party now had a leader over whom it had no control at all.

Brown, Blair plus Powell, Campbell, advertising/polling expert Philip Gould and Peter Mandelson made up virtually the whole of New Labour. The jury is still out on the relative significance of these individuals. Powell seems the least significant - a technician who came aboard long after the ship had sailed. Campbell has become a very significant player and was sometimes referred to as 'the real deputy prime minister' during Blair's first term. (The portrait of him and Blair in the *Rory Bremner Show* on Channel 4, with Campbell bossing Blair, is apparently close to reality.) But he has had no discernible influence on policy.

Peter Mandelson's significance in all this is more difficult to estimate. As Director of Communications under Neil Kinnock he was undoubtedly important in that period and had a major, though by most accounts not overwhelming, hand in the (losing) election campaigns of 1987 and 1992. As Tony Blair's confidant over the post-Kinnock period, he has certainly been significant in the wooing and partial co-opting of the British media on the faction's behalf, especially after Blair took over from John Smith. (Smith didn't like him and ignored him.) Mandelson's influence was partially the result of his experience at London Weekend Television in the early 1980s where he learned how the media and politics interact, and where he created a network in the London media which was useful later.

On the other hand, how difficult was it to sell New Labour? After 1992, and especially after Smith's death and the arrival of Blair as leader of the party in 1994, the story sold itself. The Tories were going to lose the next election, the next Prime Minister would be Blair and the New Labour group was ditching the old Labour Party and its policies. That New Labour was anti-union, pro-business, pro-NATO and pro-low corporate and personal taxes, was a message the media's managers and owners were keen to hear and pass on to their audience. No doubt Mandelson had become skilled at doling out stories to journalists and getting oceans of favourable coverage, but the Conservatives were in disarray and the political journalists had an unlimited appetite for gossip emanating from the Labour leader's office.

Mandelson held two significant positions in Blair's Governments, as Secretary of State for Northern Ireland and then for Trade and Industry. He seems to have achieved little and had to resign from both posts. There are no specific policies with his name on them, though he was the main New Labour figure behind the costly fiasco of the Millennium Dome.[7]

In 1995 and 1996 it was obvious that Labour would win the next election and the New Labour group set out to do two things. Ensure that Labour won the next election, and then make Labour, not the Conservatives, the party which represented the interests of big business. Though much of the old Tory funding remained loyal, sections of business responded warmly to the overtures from Labour. Their motives were mixed. For those who sought more enthusiastic British membership of the European Union, or membership of the approaching European Single Currency area, Labour seemed a better bet than the Tories with their strong EU-phobic wing. For others it was simply good business to get close to the next Government, especially one as naive about business as Labour. While the Conservatives had a fund-raising and laundering system which went back to the early years of the century, this was new ground for Labour, and it needed to create its own network.[8] As the election of 1997 approached, smartly-suited young men and women, but mostly men, in the employ of the Labour Party or from the offices of its leading figures, peeled off to start or join lobbying companies to collect the money from business.[9]

The Tories were consistently way behind Labour in the polls as a result of the ERM fiasco of 1992 (and the recession which the pound's brief ERM membership had engendered), and their internal and public division over the EEC/EU. But the New Labour group were willing to take no chances. They believed that their success or failure could be determined by the media. They had all been involved in the losses in 1987 and 1992, and believed that the hostility of the media played a major factor, particularly in 1992. Having ditched all the economic policies which distinguished them from the Conservative Party, they set out to persuade the media - who would pass the message on to their readers and viewers - that the changes were real and permanent. Labour was once again 'electable' because there was no hidden left agenda, no opposition to NATO plans, the unions would have no influence and the economy would be run along the lines dictated by the City.

At the heart of their concerns was Rupert Murdoch and *The Sun*. After the 1992 election it was widely believed, not least by Neil Kinnock and those around him, that Labour had lost the election because of *The Sun*'s unremittingly hostile coverage of Labour, and of Kinnock in particular. To prevent this happening again, the New Labour group wooed Murdoch and his executives. Anything they wanted, New Labour would deliver.[10] Tony Blair flew to Australia to pledge his allegiance at a meeting of News International's executives in 1995. This was 'an extraordinary act of fealty.'[11]

But it paid off. From late 1995 onwards the Murdoch papers were, at worst, neutral towards Labour. Former tabloid journalist, then Blair's press secretary, Alastair Campbell began writing articles to go under Blair's name in the Murdoch papers. The first appeared in *The News Of The World*:

> 'Other papers woke up to the ease with which Blair articles could be obtained. Soon the Leader of the Opposition became the most prolific journalist in Fleet St, by far... It was not long before the burden of writing his [Blair] comment pieces became too great for Campbell alone, and he was forced to farm out the work to junior members of the press office.'[12]

Labour's media monitoring and briefing machine at Millbank Tower, based on the Clinton campaign's version, had a wonderful time after 1995. The recession produced by joining the ERM, and their subsequent ejection from it, lost the Conservatives their fundamental appeal to the electorate - their claim to economic competence. It didn't matter that post-ERM under Kenneth Clarke as Chancellor, with a competitive currency, the economy began turning round in 1995 and 1996. Nobody took any notice. With office in sight, Labour presented a unified face to the media with all internal divisions suppressed. The Conservatives were hopelessly and publicly divided, fighting over Europe and over the coming leadership campaign after John Major led the Tories to inevitable defeat. The media, which had so ruthlessly hunted and attacked the Labour Party in the 1980s, now turned on the Conservative Party, with the Labour media people steering, cajoling and bullying on the sidelines.

In 1997 Tony Blair finally led Labour to victory on the back of an election campaign which had actually begun in 1994.

Notes

1. See the profile of Michael Levy in *The Daily Express*, 26 June 2000.

2. Geoffrey Alderman, 'Playing Tennis With Blair,' *The Jewish Quarterly*, Autumn 1997.

3. *The Sunday Times*, 2 July 2000. For 'dazzled by his drive and religious commitment' I would read 'supported Israel.'

4. In most, e.g. John Rentoul, *Tony Blair* (London: Little,Brown, 1995), page 390, the money came from Barry Cox, Peter Mandelson's erstwhile boss at London Weekend Television (LWT). On the LWT network see Andy Beckett, 'A World Apart,' *The Guardian* (*Weekend*), 4 September 1999.

5. John Lloyd, *The New Statesman*, 27 February 1998.

6. It was reported in *The Sunday Telegraph*, 25 July 1999, that Blair tried to make Levy a Minister in the Foreign and Commonwealth Office (FCO). This would have been a stunning coup by the Israelis but it was resisted by the Foreign Secretary, at the behest, presumably, of the traditionally pro-Arab FCO. Instead, Levy became Blair's personal envoy to the Middle East - to no great effect thus far.

On Blair's dislike of Labour see Philip Gould, *The Unfinished Revolution* (London: Little,Brown, 1998), page 216, where he quotes Blair: 'I will never compromise. I would rather be beaten and leave politics than bend to the party. I am going to take the party on.' Also, in Geoffrey Wheatcroft's 'Peter's Friend,' *The Observer*, 4 February 2001, Wheatcroft quotes Blair's friend, the novelist Robert Harris: 'You have to remember that the great passion of Tony's life is his hatred of the Labour Party.'

If he hated the party, why did he join it? One report in an (alas) undated cutting I have, from *The Daily Mail* circa 1997, I think, has a purported barrister friend saying he asked why Blair, no lefty, had joined Labour. Blair replied that he thought he would rise faster in Labour. Ah, the authentic ringing tone of a pure careerist move! On the other hand, this from *The Daily Mail*? 'The Forger's Gazette,' as Michael Foot called it? Maybe...

7. There has been a good deal on Mandelson in the media but the earlier profiles seem more interesting to me than those which followed. See, for example: Peter Lennon, 'Guarding The Good Name Of The Rose,' *The Guardian*, 2 October 1989; Donald Macintyre, 'Not Spin Doctor But

Counsellor,' *The Independent*, 29 July 1996; and Seamus Milne, 'The Leader's Little Helper,' *The Guardian* (*Weekend*), 11 February 1995. Paul Routledge's biography *Mandy: The Unauthorised Biography Of Peter Mandelson* (London: Pocket Books, 1999) assembles all the known fragments on Mandelson's early career to suggest that he has had some kind of secret relationship with MI6. I also suspect this but, like Routledge, do not have the evidence.

On his later escapades among the rich see *Punch* 47 and 48, 1998, and www.bilderberg.org/1999.htm#Eye.

8. On the Tories' money-raising history see Colin Challen, *The Price Of Power* (London: Vision, 1998).

9. This is too big a subject to tackle here but see: Paul Richards, 'The Millbank Mafia,' *Punch* 52, 1998; Tom Baldwin, 'Campaign Staff Cash In With New Contacts,' *The Sunday Telegraph*, 1 June 1997; Mark Watts and Rob Evans, 'Who Really Influences New Labour?' *The New Statesman*, 26 July 1999; and Greg Palast, 'The Project,' *The Ecologist*, Vol. 30, No.2, April 2000.

New at the game, Labour's bagmen were not very good at keeping their mouths shut and blew the gaff when the first enterprising journalist, Greg Palast, turned up posing as a rich American businessman with money to spend, triggering the 'cash for access' scandal. See: Greg Palast's report in *The Observer*, 12 July 1998; *The Sunday Telegraph* of the same day; and Luke Harding, 'From Chorley To The Charmed Circle,' *The Guardian*, 7 July 1998. This last piece contains a list of lobbyists associated with the Labour Party. Greg Palast's writing on this and other subjects is at www.gregpalast.com/ Palast is very good indeed.

10. This is described by Peter Oborne, *Alastair Campbell: New Labour And The Rise Of The Media Class* (London: Aurum Press, 1999), pages 140-4.

11. Oborne (see note 10), page 141. In 1998 it was Chancellor of the Exchequer, Gordon Brown, who made the pilgrimage to address the executives of Murdoch's News Corporation, on this occasion in Idaho, USA. See Tom Baldwin's 'Focus' profile of Gordon Brown, *The Sunday Telegraph*, 26 July 1998.

12. Oborne (see note 10), page 143.

7. In Love With America

'New Labour's solution has been to replace simplistic anti-Americanism with a vulgar Atlanticism, obliging Britain to bow to every American concern, no matter how trivial'

- David Clark, aide to former
Foreign Secretary Robin Cook,
The Observer, 15 July 2001.

New Labour leaders think of themselves as pragmatists though they don't use the word (in Labour Party circles the word is forever contaminated by its association with Harold Wilson). "We are interested in what works," says Tony Blair. And he has said, "We are beyond ideology." Does Blair know that 'beyond ideology' was one of the key slogans in the CIA's psy-war efforts to prevent socialism in Europe after World War Two? Probably not; and he wouldn't be interested.

In the 1950s the appeal of 'beyond ideology' was obvious. Europe had been wrecked by the war; the US was producing about half the world's Gross Domestic Product (GDP) in 1945. How wonderful the East Coast of the US must have seemed then to the Labour politicians taking the American Government-funded trips across the Atlantic. And everywhere they went they heard the same message. Capitalism (American production methods) had cracked it. Redistribution, let alone fuddy-duddy old socialism, will not be necessary to solve the problems of the world. No more class struggle. No more conflict. A rising tide floats all the boats. It is the end of ideology.

Now we are being governed by another group of America fans. Fifty years after their Gaitskellite forbears in the American tendency in Labour, they too believe the Americans have cracked it. Neo-liberalism, as they see it, is not only unavoidable but correct. For the second time this century America is triumphant and, would you believe it, we have Labour politicians who have got the message. Blair and Brown look at the vast, mineral-rich, largely empty continent of America and see things we should copy here on this overcrowded island. They apparently do not see the 2 million in jail, the 25,000 gunshot deaths every year, the hundreds of thousands living on the streets and the corrupt political system. They do not see the America in which the President, his brother the probable next President and the most important black leader of his time, were assassinated in 5 years, by conspiracies which have not been identified, let alone prosecuted. They do not see the America which murdered hundreds of thousands of people in Central America ('fighting for freedom and democracy') while the CIA, with permission from the Attorney General of America, turned a blind eye to the importation of cocaine by its allies in the slaughter of the populations of El Salvador, Guatemala and Nicaragua. (The events in Central America happened while Blair and Brown were Members of Parliament.) The current American tendency within Labour is simply not looking at *that* America.

In a sense the question, 'Why are they infatuated with America?' is barely worth asking. Added to the vast cultural, historical and political baggage of Anglo-American connections, in the last 40 years or so US popular culture has come to dominate UK society. Florida is now one of the leading holiday destinations for British citizens. Why should the leaders of the Labour Party be immune to America's appeal? This writer isn't. Since I was in my early teens listening to Willis Conover playing jazz on the Voice of America, most of the music I have listened to, the books I have read and the films I have watched have been American. As much as anyone I know I have been colonised by post-war American culture. But it's one thing to be smitten by bits of the culture and quite another to want to imitate its foreign, social and economic policies. The Brown/Blair group are true believers bent on imitating American policies where possible.

As is now well known, most of the leading players in New Labour, and many of their assistants, have worked or studied in America. David Miliband, Blair's head of policy, did a Masters degree at the Massachusetts Institute of Technology. Jonathan Powell, Blair's chief of staff, is a former Foreign Office official whose previous posting was in the British Embassy in Washington.[1] Ed Balls, Gordon Brown's economic adviser, studied at Harvard and was about to join the World Bank with one of his tutors at Harvard before he joined Brown. His wife, junior minister Yvette Cooper, also studied at Harvard. Marjorie Mowlam, an important member of the tendency until recently and formerly Secretary of State for Northern Ireland, did a PhD at the University of Iowa and then taught in the United States in the 1970s. Chris Smith (a Minister until 2001), David Miliband and Ed Balls were Kennedy Scholars in the USA.[2] Sue Nye, Gordon Brown's long-time personal assistant, is married to Gavyn Davies, chief economist with the American bankers Goldman Sachs and one of Labour's main economic advisers since the 1980s. Stephen Pollard, one of the back-room players in the formation of New Labour, took the 'freebie' American tour in 1994, while he was working for the Fabian Society.[3]

The entire defence team in the Blair first administration were members of, or associated with, the Trade Union Committee for European and Transatlantic Unity (TUCETU). This began as the Labour Committee for Transatlantic Unity and was set up in 1976 by Joseph Godson. Godson had been US Labour Attaché in London in the 1950s and had recruited the Gaitskellites to the point where he and party leader Gaitskell were jointly writing Labour Party policies and planning strategy against the Labour left.[4]

Peter Mandelson, Marjorie Mowlam, George Robertson (former Defence Minister now Secretary General of NATO), Chris Smith (former Heritage Minister), Elizabeth Symons (junior Foreign Office Minister in the House of Lords) and Jonathan Powell (Blair's chief of staff) have all been members of the British-American Project for a Successor Generation (BAP), the latest in the long line of American-funded networks which promote American interests and thinking among the British political elite.[5] The BAP newsletter for June/July 1997 headlined its account of the 1997 Labour Election Victory as 'Big Swing To BAP.'[6]

Tony Blair took the US Government 'freebie' tour which consists of being given a couple of briefings, a load of money and told to go and have a look. You have to work hard to not have a good time in those circumstances. Brown spends his holidays (and had his honeymoon) in New England. He was shown the wonders of neo-liberal economic theory by academics at Harvard. I have been to New England and its charms are obvious. Much of it is very rich and the countryside is beautiful. New England is Heaven on earth for many of the rich, white people who live there. But if you visit Yale University in New Haven, the menial work of servicing the (mostly) white students, is done by the poor blacks who live in the town. The New England coastline is lovely but much of it is privately owned and off-limits. In their account of Brown's first year in office Hugh Pym and Nick Kochan said, 'These holidays [in New England] gave Gordon Brown free access to American culture.' But the New England the tourist sees isn't America.[7]

On top of the general admiration of America there is an identification with the US Democratic Party. A friend of a friend of mine was in the same London Labour Party branch as Tony Blair in the early 1980s and remembers Blair even then talking of changing the Labour Party into something like the Democratic Party. (Given Blair's dislike of the Labour Party, presumably part of the appeal of the Democratic Party was the absence of ordinary members interfering with the deliberations of the elite. Democratic Senators don't have to attend constituency meetings with groups of party members who might not share their high opinion of themselves.) There had always been some links between the two parties and, when they faced the dominance of the Conservative-Republican bloc (the Thatcher and Reagan show) in the 1980s, the sense of identity grew. If the account of Labour pollster and advertising man, Philip Gould, is to be believed, it was not just on the Labour side. Gould had been visiting the Democrats since 1986 and the occasional Democratic worker came across to help Labour after that.[8] In 1992, after Labour had lost, Labour Party people went across to look at the Clinton election machine. They saw a massive system of media monitoring and briefing which was used to counter-attack the Republicans and the media bias against them. Philip Gould (*The Unfinished Revolution*, page 167) refers to that system distributing material to 200,000 media and other outlets! The visitors from London were deeply impressed by this system (and it won the election). After Blair became leader, a version of that machine was created in Millbank Tower in London, the like of which had never been seen in British politics. Also, many Democratic slogans and American policies were copied in what the American political journalist Joe Klein called 'a bizarre convergence of political ideas.'[9]

Even so, even given all the foregoing, the Blair/Brown fixation on America is odd in a way. There is a big difference between them and the American tendency in Labour that they succeeded. While the American tendency stood on the barricades of anti-Communism with its American colleagues, the central preoccupation of the previous group led by Roy Jenkins, was with Europe. This simply is not true of Blair and Brown.

"Whatever works" Blair says, but it's a lie. The Blair/Brown group are conspicuously not interested in anything happening on mainland Europe. If they were interested in the EU countries they would be studying: Holland, Denmark or Sweden for social policies; virtually any of the EU countries for how to run a railway or a health care system; Germany for how to be a middle-ranking power without much of an army or intelligence service; Portugal, Ireland, Italy or Spain for how to get EU money without implementing its more ridiculous legislation. None of this is happening. If they meant 'whatever works' they would be studying the example of New Zealand where a neo-liberal minority took over the New Zealand Labour Party, adopted all the American-inspired policies, trashed the New Zealand economy and welfare state, destroyed the party and were eventually turned out of office.[10]

'Whatever works' actually means 'whatever the Americans are doing.'[11] Peter Mandelson's biographer, Donald Macintyre, commented:

'It would be wrong to exaggerate Brown's enthusiasm for the US... Brown can hardly overlook the existence of the American underclass or the dislocation from American society felt by many blacks.'[12]

Notice Macintyre's use of 'can hardly' - he doesn't actually know if Brown does or not. Neither do I, of course, but I think Brown and Blair *are* overlooking the American 'underclass,' America's racism, its murderous foreign policy, its imperialism and its plundering of the globe's resources. Against Macintyre, Matthew d'Ancona reported:

'[Brown's] preoccupation with best practice across the Atlantic is all-consuming: one Cabinet minister told me that "the only sure way to get Gordon to listen to a policy idea is to produce an American who believes in it."'[13]

It wasn't always thus. In the 1980s it was to the German economy, not the United States, that Labour politicians turned their envious eyes. In the 1980s the German model seemed to offer growth, stability, low inflation and high living standards. The German model has been abandoned. If you asked New Labour why, eventually they might cough up a spokesperson who would tell you about high unemployment, the 'sclerotic' state of the European economy, not enough job creation and unsustainable welfare burdens. But mostly he or she would talk about jobs. Since New Labour believe it is impossible to raise business and income taxes, it is unable to promise much Government activity. Not nothing, let's be fair, but not much.[14] The American economic model is perceived as being 'more dynamic,' i.e. creating more jobs, than the European model. (The rival far Eastern economic models are simply not considered.)

But does the American system create more jobs? US unemployment figures are distorted by the absence from the figures of some 2 million male members of the working class, mostly black, many of whom would be unemployed, who are in prison.[15] In a letter to *The Guardian* (9 July 1999) about what he called the US 'penal economy,' Professor David Downes pointed out that while the US has an official unemployment rate of 4.5%, if the number of men in the US prison system were taken into account, the unemployment rate would rise to between 6.5% and 8.5%, depending on whether or not the count included the penal system's staff! And this is not markedly better than the unemployment rates in the 'sclerotic' EU economies.

Nor is it obvious that the British and American economies can be meaningfully compared.

> 'The Government is trying to build American-style economic dynamism on top of a foundation of European stability. The problem is that, in a continuing convulsion of wilful innocence, it misunderstands the nature of America's dynamism. Yes, it comes from technology. Yes, it comes from a culture of risk-taking, where failure doesn't equal humiliation. But it also comes from the US's mammoth internal market, its steady stream of legal and illegal immigrants, and its bully-boy tactics in dictating the terms of world trade and financial flows.'[16]

Labour's focus on American-style policies goes back to the decisions taken in the late 1980s and early 1990s about economic policy. Between 1988 and 1992 the Labour leadership rejected the post-war consensus that the state could, and had an obligation to, manage the economy to create full employment for its citizens. The Labour leadership was persuaded that the best the state could manage was the creation of economic stability (defined by them as low inflation) and a certain amount of fiddling around the edges: education, training, infrastructure. The rest was up to the dynamic nature of capitalism. In the same period the Labour leadership was persuaded that it could no longer try to use the state to redistribute wealth and income to reduce poverty, as the British electorate simply would not pay the taxes required. (The loss in 1992 was perceived by Labour to be largely down to the success of the 'Labour tax bombshell' campaign by the Conservatives.) Poverty reduction would come, if it came at all, chiefly through getting low income groups into work. In effect 'the modernisers' adopted Thatcherism, but could hardly use the name. They adopted American neo-liberalism as a more palatable way of dressing it up for themselves and the party's members.

At the core of the big Labour policy shift in 1988/9 is the belief that the nation state is powerless against the global economy. But while it is certainly true, as the 1992 ERM fiasco showed, that nation states are unable to defend currency rates which the international money markets regard as unrealistic, where is the evidence to support the view that the nation state can no longer manage its own economy? The stock response is reference to the 'French failure' in 1983, when the Mitterand Government tried to expand the economy in a pretty traditional demand management fashion. Trying to expand their economy, the French Government began spending money. The increased demand generated by their spending increased imports which threatened the value of the Franc against the Deutschmark. At this point classical expansionist theory said let the Franc devalue. But the Franc was in the Exchange Rate Mechanism (ERM) and, while devaluation within the ERM was possible, the French Government was pursuing a policy of '*Franc fort*,' strong Franc, in competition with the Deutschmark, and chose to give up the domestic expansion it had embarked on rather than see the Franc devalue. Although this merely demonstrates what everyone knew, that if the domestic economy is expanded it may be necessary to devalue in the short term, this has been almost universally interpreted in Labour circles, especially pro-EEC Labour circles, as demonstrating the impossibility of unilateral economic action by nation states.[17] But even the simplest accounts of demand management economics (which is what 'Keynesianism' actually means; few of those using these terms, including this writer, have actually read Keynes) acknowledge that it may be necessary to abandon attempts to maintain fixed currency rates if expansion is pursued.[18] (The real mystery of the French expansion in 1983 is how they thought they could have expansion *and* a '*Franc fort*.')

But while the French failure looms large in the we-are-powerless Labour modernising mind, the experience of the British economy after being forced out of the ERM in 1992 by the same 'global market forces,' does not. This is not entirely a surprise as it doesn't fit their theories. When the UK joined the ERM in 1990 both main political parties were agreed that this was a guaranteed anti-inflation device. For over a year the Labour leadership badgered the Conservative Government to join this wonderful system. Since the economic policies of the Conservative Party were being written by the City of London, the pound entered the ERM at a rate which could be sustained only by higher interest rates than the rest of the EU. Good for the City; bad for the rest of the economy. Cue the second, major, Conservative-induced recession in a decade, and cue Labour's guaranteed win at the next election. But, as Mrs Thatcher was wont to say, you can't buck the market; and the world's currency dealers concluded that at 2.95 Deutschmark, the ERM entry level, the pound was seriously overvalued. This was a view shared by a wide section of British economists and, we are now led to believe, despite their silence on the subject at the time, by the Labour Shadow Cabinet.[19] The currency dealers knew that the British Government was obliged to 'defend' the value of the pound and the Bank of England proceeded to do so in the usual way (giving its reserves away to the currency dealers) before it recognised defeat and withdrew from the ERM.

The value of Sterling duly fell but none of the predictions of economic disaster turned out to be true. Inflation did not shoot up, domestic production expanded with the more competitive pound, exports grew and unemployment fell. *In direct contradiction of everything Labour's economics spokespersons apparently believed*, the relatively good economic position inherited by the Blair Government in 1997 is a consequence of the British economy leaving the ERM. (Which may explain Gordon Brown's manifest reluctance to rush into the Single Currency.)

We Are Powerless

The acid test for Labour 'modernisers' has become how completely you accept the powerlessness-of-Government thesis. The thesis sounds immediately plausible to those, like New Labour economics spokespersons, with little economic knowledge. It is what they keep reading in the newspapers and being told by their advisers from the City.

In *The Independent On Sunday* of 15 January 1996, Alastair Darling, Gordon Brown's deputy at the Treasury in the first term, was quoted as saying, "It is not up to the Government to say that the banks can only make so much profit." Here the recent convert to the wonders of the market shows that he hasn't grasped that banks are *not* just another set of businesses to be left to their own devices. And it certainly *used* to be 'up to the Government,' even Conservative Chancellor of the Exchequer Geoffrey Howe imposed a windfall tax on the banks in 1981. But that was back in those far-off days before the Government handed over power to set interest rates (perhaps the most powerful single economic tool and the surest means of regulating how much banks earn) to the people who stand to gain by putting interest rates up! Bankers are always 'inflation hawks.' They don't mind putting up the cost of borrowing because that's how they make their bonuses.

Just before the 1997 General Election, Roy Hattersley wrote in his *Guardian* column of meeting one of the then Labour shadow economics team, who told him that in the new global economy it was not possible for a Government to increase taxes.[20] On his visit to the beleaguered Bill Clinton in February 1998, Tony Blair told *Guardian* journalist and long-time New Labour ally, Martin Kettle, of the 'five clear principles of the centre-left.' The first of these was:

> '...stable management and economic prudence *because of the global economy*.'[21] (Emphasis added.)

The powerlessness thesis also has the advantage of being a popular line with Labour supporters of the European Union who can argue, as the Labour Party has done since they became Euro-enthusiasts, that we need Europeanwide action and, preferably, a single currency to control capital ('the speculators'). Just over a decade ago Gordon Brown sold ERM membership to the Parliamentary Labour Party, most of whom knew even less about economics than he does, as a mechanism to frustrate the speculators. To my knowledge, he has never publicly commented on what lessons he drew from Sterling's ejection from the ERM after the speculators had made several billion pounds profit from the British tax-payer.

The striking thing about New Labour is the way they have managed to convince themselves that the free market is the only possible (or successful) model when that proposition is immediately falsified by the experience of, for example, Norway or the Asian variants of corporatist, nationalist, restrictive, trade barrier and exchange control-laden economies. The so-called Asian 'tiger' economies had developed and grown in defiance of Anglo-American, neo-liberal, free market theories.[22]

Why have New Labour leaders adopted the powerlessness thesis? In part, it is simply that they are in the grip of theories and exclude information which might challenge them. The theories are reinforced by being those currently approved of by their mentors in the United States and the British financial establishment. As far as alternative views are perceived, they are offered by people who, for one reason or another, are regarded by New Labour as either discredited, such as the Labour left, or beyond the pale, such as the Tory Europhobes. I also think that New Labour politicians rather *welcome* the belief that they are powerless against the world's financial markets. Since they are powerless, a range of things that Labour leaders used to try to deliver (growth, economic justice, redistribution) have ceased to be rational expectations of them. Nothing can be done short of Europeanwide action, and maybe not even then.[23] Life is infinitely easier for Labour economic ministers when all they have to do is follow the neo-liberal line coming from their City advisors.

Blair and Brown give every indication of being as naive as they appear.[24] They really do believe this stuff. Forgive me if this is repetitive but, like others, I still have trouble grasping how they could possibly see US-dominated globalisation as the solution. Do we really have to recite highlights of the post-war encounter between the Third World and the United States to these people? A little matter of several million dead people in Vietnam, Cambodia and Laos, for example? How about Chile? Guatemala? How about 'Blowtorch Bob' d'Aubuisson, the Americans' proxy killer in El Salvador? Do we really have to recritique the IMF and World Bank as the agents of imperialism? I have to occasionally remind myself that this New Labour *thing* isn't a great con, with Gordon Brown about to nip into a phone box, rip his shirt off and reveal himself as Social Justice Man.

Can they really believe that the multinational drug companies are just itching to sell their products at cost price to the Third World?

Apparently so.

Can they really believe that the West's bankers are willing to write off the debts owed them by the Third World?

Apparently so.

Can they really believe that British/multinational companies feel some moral obligation to invest in the infrastructure of Britain?

Apparently so.

Can they really believe more American-style 'freedom' is what the developing world needs?

Definitely so.

Look, for example, at the absurd piece co-authored by Gordon Brown and Clare Short, 'Our Answer To Protesters' (the protesters being those in Genoa in July 2001) which announces, *inter alia*,

> '...the IMF, the World Bank, the UN [United Nations] and the OECD [Organisation for Economic Cooperation and Development] - and individual Governments - have signed up to challenging 2015 targets: that poverty across the globe is cut by half; that every one of the 120m children in the world currently denied primary education receive it; and that infant mortality is cut to one third of its present level.'[25]

As if the wishes of organisations such as the OECD or the UN carried any weight with the global corporations! As if signing up to targets 15 years down the road, after all the signatories have retired or moved on to other jobs, means something!

There was an ad in *The Economist*, 26 May 2001, for a Trade Policy Programme Co-ordinator for Africa in the Department for International Development, for which Ms Short is the Minister. This tells us that applicants:

> 'must bring an understanding of globalisation and development and the links between trade and poverty reduction.'

The ideology of globalisation is now institutionalised in that department. It is official *Labour* Government policy that poverty reduction in the world is soluble only by giving the developing countries more of the US-led imperialism which dropped them in the mire in the first place!

The seriously excellent Gregory Palast noted in a piece in May 2000 that while the US in trade politics were the predictable hypocrites (preaching free trade but practising domestic protection when it suits them), the Labour Government were far more willing to accommodate the wishes of global business.[26] New Labour's leaders are zealots who lecture the world on how to make globalisation work better and faster. In July and August 2001, Gordon Brown called for Europe and the United States to form 'a transatlantic alliance for prosperity' by knocking down the remaining tariff walls between their economies,[27] while Tony Blair lectured the EU countries that they had to copy America[28] then praised Mexico for embracing free trade.[29] I wonder what the leaders of the other EU countries thought about being lectured by the leader of a country which has a failing public health care system, a failing rail network and cannot attract enough teachers to educate its children?

In the emulation of America nothing is too absurd, no comparison is too specious. After the 2001 election, Brown noted that the rate of formation of small businesses was lower in the UK than it is in America. Not only that, Brown had discovered that 'the rate of small businesses formed in the poorer areas was just one sixth of the more prosperous areas.' An astounding revelation! The poor don't start businesses? Would this have something to do with, er, lack of money? To rectify this we apparently need 'an enterprise culture genuinely open to all...,' whatever that might look like. Thus, the semantic journey away from the old Labour Party is complete. Talk of equality, with its implications of redistribution, gave way to talk of equality of opportunity in the later 1950s under the impact of the first wave of naive fans of America. In the early 1990s, talk of equality of opportunity was abandoned because it sounded too radical and Brown talked of 'opportunity for all' for a while. Now that has given way to 'an enterprise culture open to all.'[30]

With the infatuation with America comes a naive infatuation with the market economy. This cabinet, without any business experience, truly believes the market is magic and all problems can be resolved by letting the consumer choose. In a piece about Railtrack and the chaos of the privatised rail network, the journalist Christian Woolmar reported thus:

'Capitalism functions best when there is a clear product to market, sold in the face of competition from rivals, and the reward for more investment is the ability to increase output thus boosting sales. Railtrack fits none of this model. Its raison d'être is to provide "train paths" for the operators but these are in limited supply since much of the network is full and the cost of investment prohibitive. I tried recently to explain this at great length to a highly intelligent senior Government minister but he utterly failed to understand that Railtrack is different from Coca-Cola.'[31]

The last British politician in office who was as naive as this lot about business was Edward Heath, who thought they would all be behind him in his push to remake Britain as Germany and got cross when he found them dragging their feet.[32]

In the beginning these policies were presented as 'the Third Way.' The first two ways were capitalism and socialism, so the third way is...? Capitalism fronted by a notionally socialist party? The concept was fairly quickly ditched by Blair/Brown after a deluge of intellectual contempt and general hilarity. This seemed to show the cynics amongst us that we were right. There was little more to 'the Third Way' than there was to 'Britain: A Young Country.' Just more slogans and 'branding.' Advertising guff in, advertising guff out. In fact, it was worse than this.

What was on offer was a kind of parody of corporatism. The old corporatist model of the 1960s and 1970s, from which Blair/Brown are so keen to distance themselves, was a three-legged stool: the unions; the managers of capital; and the Government. The new model excludes the unions and is a putative partnership between capital and the Government. The unions? Embarrassing hangovers from the bad old days of old Labour and tax and spend Government. Now Government and business, private and public, will work together to rebuild British society. But the new model rests on beliefs about corporate identity with the UK and its fate, which are foolish and naive in the extreme. These beliefs are strikingly at odds with New Labour's belief in globalisation. For, at the bottom of the theory (if we can call it that) of globalisation is the belief that it is a good thing, *the best possible thing*, for companies to pursue profit wherever it is highest. Why then should the global companies give a monkey's about social conditions in the UK (or anywhere else)?

This new model was offered to the corporate world which provided people for a vast array of 'task forces' on various areas whose reports will end up in waste bins all over Whitehall.[33] The corporate world took what it could get, notably access to the assets still owned by the public sector, and has given almost nothing back. Companies will do a bit if it makes for good PR (responsible, caring for the environment; computer vouchers for schools, that sort of thing) because they've got PR budgets which cover it. But beyond that, they will only do things when there are sales and market share to be gained.[34] And why would it be any other way?

Notes

1. Ken Coates and Michael Barratt Brown suggested in their book *The Blair Revelation* (Nottingham: Spokesman, 1996) that Powell's job in the British embassy in Washington concealed a role as the liaison officer between British intelligence and the CIA, but they have no evidence. Powell's career summary, as given in *The Diplomatic Service List* for 1995, contains nothing from which to infer an intelligence role. He was born in 1956 and joined the FCO (Foreign and Commonwealth Office) in 1979. Since then: he was Third later Second Secretary in Lisbon, 1981; Second later First Secretary at the FCO, London; UK delegate to CDE Stockholm, 1986; UK delegate at the CSCE in Vienna, 1986; First Secretary FCO, London, 1989; and then First Secretary (Chancery) Washington, 1991. His role in America has been elsewhere described as Political Officer which, in my limited experience, usually does not denote a cover role for MI6. They may turn out to be right but they have no evidence.

2. Peter Hennessy, 'The View From Here,' *The Independent* (*Education*), 1 May 1997.

3. See Stephen Pollard, 'Labour Should Follow Bush, Not Sneer At Him,' *The Sunday Telegraph*, 29 April 2001. Pollard was the author of an influential study of the perceptions of Labour by the southern middle class, 'Southern Discomfort.'

4. On TUCETU see David Osler, 'New Labour, New Atlanticism: US And Tory Intervention In The Unions Since The 1970s,' *Lobster* 33, June 1997. TUCETU is now funded by NATO.

5. See Tom Easton's 'The British-American Project For The Successor Generation,' *Lobster* 33. BAP have now dropped 'For The Successor Generation' from their organisation's title, apparently as a result of Easton pointing out that the phrase first appeared after a meeting between Ronald Reagan, Rupert Murdoch and Sir James Goldsmith in 1983. BAP deny that its formation had anything to do with that meeting and, given the political orientation of its co-instigator, the industrialist Sir Charles Villiers, I am inclined to believe it.

6. BAP published a pamphlet to counter the view of it given in the first big piece about it in *Lobster* (see preceding note), Martin Vander Weyer,

A Common Bond: The Origins Of The British-American Project (no date but 1998 or 1999). In it one of its founders, Nick Butler of BP, tells us, he 'originally thought of the Project as a way of putting Labour people like himself in touch with American ideas - but on economic and social issues.' Butler, it was announced shortly after the 2001 election, is to oversee the introduction of private sector money into the public services.

7. Hugh Pym and Nick Kochan, *Gordon Brown: The First Year In Power* (London: Bloomsbury, 1998), page 113.

8. Philip Gould, *The Unfinished Revolution* (London: Little,Brown, 1998), pages 162/3. After the 1997 election, Gould and the Democratic Party pollster, Stan Greenberg, set up a 'transatlantic consultancy.' Anne McElvoy, 'Fanatic Of The Focus Group,' *The Independent*, 22 July 2000.

9. Joe Klein, 'The Party's Over,' *The Guardian 2*, 24 May 2001, page 2. Klein wrote *Primary Colours*, the *roman à clef* about the Bill Clinton campaign for the Democratic nomination, subsequently filmed with John Travolta as the Clintonesque character.

10. The best account of the New Zealand version of American neo-liberal economics is Jane Kelsey, *Economic Fundamentalism* (London: Pluto Press, 1995).

11. Or, maybe, the Australians. There is some evidence of New Labour picking up ideas from Australia. That's another vast, empty continent like the United States, dominated by American social and economic thinking.

12. 'Why Is Mr Brown So Fascinated By America?' *The Independent*, 8 August 2000. Notice Macintyre's phrase 'underclass and... the *dislocation* from American society felt by many blacks.' *Woke up this morning, felt dis-lo-cated...* doesn't make it, does it? Macintyre would have his readers see the words underclass and dislocation instead of poverty and racism. Macintyre has been close to New Labour, especially Peter Mandelson, whose biography he wrote. Part of the New Labour programme is the attempt to 'rebrand' things like poverty and racism into not-so-nasty-sounding things like 'social exclusion.' In the 1950s sociologists 'rediscovered' poverty in Britain. In the 1990s they attempted to rebrand it. This must be ironic...

13. *The Sunday Telegraph*, 14 January 2001.

14. The extraordinary and blatant rip-off which is the Private Finance Initiative is an expression of the same thing. Unwilling to raise taxes to the level of the rest of the EU, the only way Labour can deliver on its promises to improve the public services is to invite the private sector to do it. Since the private sector knows this, it can secure ludicrously generous contracts from the Government.

15. An Associated Press story on 27 August 2001 reported that: 'The number of adults behind bars, on parole or on probation reached a record 6.47 million in 2000 - or one in 32 American adults, the Government reported yesterday... Jails and prisons held 30 percent of the adults in the corrections system, or 1,933,503.'

In Britain in the 1980s the unemployment figures were faked by allowing a vast expansion in the number of people taken off the unemployment register as suffering from long-term illness. This continues today. See, for example, the report in 'Sickness Claims Mask Jobless Rate,' *The Guardian*, 5 September 2001, in which David Webster told a meeting of the British Association for the Advancement of Science that perhaps 7% of the UK workforce is off the unemployment register because they are registered as long-term sick.

16. Peter Koenig, 'Wake From Your American Dream, Gordon,' *The Independent*, 14 March 1999.

17. For an example of the left's interpretation of the French experience proving the impossibility of national action see Paul Anderson and Nyta Mann, *Safety First: The Making Of New Labour* (London: Granta Books, 1997), page 80. For the contrary view see Seamus Milne, 'A French Lesson For The Left,' *Tribune*, 26 March 1993.

18. If Keynes were alive he might well proclaim that he isn't a Keynesian, just as Marx famously said, 'Je ne suis pas Marxiste.'

19. Neil Kinnock's assistant at the time, Neil Stewart, commented that the reason Kinnock did not express his belief that pound was overvalued was, "It's a dickhead says it before the Tories." John Rentoul, *Tony Blair* (London: Little,Brown, 1995), page 267. This is worth spelling out. At face value, the story is this: although Labour wanted British entry into the ERM, and although they saw that the pound had gone into the ERM at an unsustainably high level, rather than be perceived to be calling for devaluation of Sterling, Labour spokespersons said nothing - and so assisted in the failure of the pound in the ERM.

20. Hattersley declined to tell me the name of this person. This was an echo of Tony Blair's 1996 comment in Japan that, "We also recognise that in a global economy... our tax rates need to be internationally as well as nationally competitive." Tony Blair, *New Britain* (London: Fourth Estate, 1996), page 123.

21. *The Guardian*, 7 February 1998.

22. This paragraph was written for *Prawn Cocktail Party* just before the 1998 collapse of the so-called Asian 'tiger' economies. The collapse is chiefly the result of those economies *reducing* the restrictions which used

to exist, in pursuit of the western free market model. This encouraged speculation (aka 'investment') by the Euro-American financial sectors, with the usual disastrous results. See, for example, the brisk, clear account in chapter 9 of Chalmers Johnson's *Blowback: The Costs And Consequences Of American Empire* (London: Little,Brown, 2000). On Norway see Larry Elliot in *The Guardian*, 6 April 1998.

23. As the corporations extend their reach so the trade union bureaucrats stretch their rhetoric to match. In the late 1970s and 1980s they talked of Europeanwide action but never managed to deliver much of it. In 1996 General Secretary of the TUC and Bilderberg meeting participant John Monks called for '*world works councils* for each major international company,' *The Guardian*, 31 January 1996. (Emphasis added.) International capitalism did not noticeably tremble at this absurd prospect.

Against the nation-state-is-powerless thesis see, for example: Larry Elliott and Dan Atkinson, *The Age Of Insecurity* (London: Verso, 1998), pages 260-264; Martin Wolf, 'Far From Powerless,' *The Financial Times*, 13 May 1997; Larry Elliot, 'Grand National Idea Produces Winners,' *The Guardian*, 20 October 1997; 'Don't Be Fooled: Multinationals Do Not Rule The World,' *The Independent On Sunday*, 12 January 1997; and Paul Hirst, 'Globaloney,' *Prospect*, February 1996.

24. In his profile of Blair in *The Sunday Telegraph*, 3 June 2001, Matthew d'Ancona wrote this: 'In his dealings with EU heads of Government, Downing Street aides say that he has learned - bitterly and *to his astonishment* - that the force of his arguments are not enough.' (Emphasis added.) Granted 'his aides' isn't much of a source, but still, a middle-aged politician who had to learn that it isn't about arguments?

25. *The Guardian*, 4 July 2001. See also Clare Short's banal attempt to elaborate her thesis that globalisation-is-good-for-the world's-poor in 'The Challenge Of Our Age,' *The New Statesman*, 16 August 1999.

26. 'Tony Rushes In Where Bill Fears To Tread,' *The Observer*, 21 May 2000.

27. Charlotte Denny, 'WTO Takes Reality Check,' *The Guardian*, 26 July 2001.

28. *The Guardian*, 31 July 2001.

29. *The Guardian*, 3 August 2001.

30. 'My Maggie Mission,' *The Daily Mail*, 19 June 2001.

31. 'The Terminal Failure Of Railtrack,' *The Guardian*, 7 June 2001.

32. 'Whatever Mr Blair might think about the leaders of Old Labour, at least they had no such illusions about the capacities of the average British

businessman.' Quoted from Ross McKibbin, 'Make Enemies And Influence People,' *London Review Of Books*, 20 July 2000.

33. On the task forces see Stuart Weir, 'The City Has Taken Over The Quangos Under New Labour,' *The Independent*, 23 November 1998, and Rosie Waterhouse and Richard Woods, 'Labour's Task Force Kings,' *The Sunday Times*, 21 November 1999.

34. On the corporate/political connections under New Labour see the important book by George Monbiot, *The Captive State* (London: Macmillan, 2000), the commentary on it in Michael Barratt Brown's *The Captive State; How Labour Was Taken Over By Capital* (Nottingham: Spokesman Books, 2001) and the various essays on the subject by Greg Palast at his Website: www.gregpalast.com/

8. Into Office

'It is scarcely credible that Britain should once again be cruci-
fied on an excessively high exchange rate.'

- Wynne Godley,
The Observer (*Business*),
23 August 1998, page 2.

By the time Labour took office, Brown and Blair had promised to toe
the conservative line on economic policy: no income tax rises; no
increased public spending; no attempts to use Government to direct the
economy; and no reacquisition of the privatised state assets (the roughly
£100 billion of taxation-created assets flogged off for around £50 billion
during the Thatcher years). All talk of justice, fairness and redistribution
had been stripped from the vocabulary. They had learned the central man-
tra of neo-liberalism: private good, public bad.

Taking office in 1997, there was only one major tool left in the hands of
new Chancellor Gordon Brown, but it was the critical one, the control of
interest rates for the economy.[1] This last lever was duly surrendered to the
Bank of England on Brown's first day in office. Henceforth interest rates
were to be set by a committee chaired by the Governor of the Bank of
England and with a majority of its members employees of the Bank. They
were tasked to keep inflation at two and a half per cent using only interest
rates.[2] For Brown, converted to the neo-liberal view of the economy, set-
ting the interest rate was simply a technical issue. Should interest rates rise
or fall? Ask the experts. And who are the experts? The bankers, of course.
But Gordon, who benefits from interest rate rises? The bankers.[3] Some-
how this most banal of observations has escaped 'the Iron Chancellor.'

The consequence of the decision to let the Bank of England control
interest rates was that *absurdly*, and *incredibly*, like Mrs Thatcher in 1979,
Labour set out in 1997 with neither an interest rate policy nor an exchange
rate policy. The Bank of England's Monetary Policy Committee duly
agreed that interest rates as low as those in the Euro zone or the United
States would not maintain inflation at the target figure and they have
remained higher ever since. (That strange noise you can hear is sniggering
from the stockbroker belt round London.) Consequently, the pound has
been too high and a chorus of complaint has issued from British manufacturing as the overvalued pound began putting them out of business. This
did not deter Brown. He wanted 'stability' and 'an end to Tory boom and

bust,' which are phrases you must have heard a hundred times a year. But Brown defined 'stability' simply as low inflation. Currency instability didn't matter and didn't get onto the agenda.[4] And we had a rerun of 1980-2. Through 1998 and into 1999, as the pound remained too high under the impact of UK interest rates (almost double those in the Euro zone), the economic journalists who had spent the 1980s warning of the consequences of the high interest rate/high Sterling policy, began recycling their old articles. They needed to do little more than change the name of the Chancellor from Howe to Brown.[5]

Finally, on 10 June 1999, the Governor of the Bank of England, Eddie George, admitted that the exchange rate had finally made it onto the agenda of the Monetary Policy Committee (MPC) which he chaired, and stated that the interest rate cut of a quarter of a percent that week by the Monetary Policy Committee had been done to try and help manufacturing. But it still left UK interest rates roughly twice those in the Euro zone and Sterling did not fall. Even then Chancellor Brown was not impressed. At the same event at which Eddie George admitted the MPC was now considering the exchange rate (even though they hadn't done anything), Brown not only failed to respond to the complaints from the domestic economy, he warned of the dangers of having an exchange rate target.

> 'Anyone who thinks that dropping the inflation target to replace it with an exchange rate target, or running inflation and exchange rate targets at the same time is the right way to achieve domestic stability is failing to learn the lessons of the 1980s.'[6]

Notice how Brown rejects a solution to a question the manufacturing sector was *not* asking. The exporters being crippled by the high value of the pound were *not* suggesting that 'running inflation and exchange rate targets at the same time is the right way to achieve domestic stability.' There were simply pointing out that the pound was so high they were going out of business! Nor is it clear which 'lessons of the 1980s' he is thinking of. Certainly not the lessons of the early 1980s when Thatcher and Howe followed a policy identical to Brown's, with the same consequences – the destruction of manufacturing jobs.

After all the policy-making and policy-changing of the 1980s and early 1990s, *New Labour's economic policy is essentially Thatcherism mark 1.* Superficially, it appears different but only because 'controlling the money supply' is no longer considered an intermediate target en route to controlling inflation. And since Brown inherited much lower inflation than existed in 1979, the Monetary Policy Committee has not yet had to be as savage as Thatcher and Howe were in the early 1980s.[7] But the policy remains the same... We will 'control' inflation by putting up interest rates, i.e. by making people unemployed. And that is, chiefly, by making people unemployed in manufacturing.

As in the 1980s, the prosperous, City-driven greater London area can experience growth while chunks of the rest of the country are in recession. In May 1999 the TUC reported that in the 106 constituencies where manufacturing employed more than 30% of the workforce, half had recorded a rise in unemployment in the previous six months.[8] As I was writing this paragraph the BBC news announced at the beginning of August 2001, that the manufacturing sector of the British economy was officially in recession, mainly because the pound is overvalued at the same time that UK interest rates are higher than those in the Euro zone and the USA. The same old story: the City does well, manufacturing does badly.

All of this is being done in pursuit of policies which now come under the rubric of 'the Washington consensus,' i.e. American-style neo-liberalism. But these policies were adopted by Labour under John Smith as Shadow Chancellor (with Brown as his deputy) when they were quite specifically the policies sought by the City of London. The City's well-being is top of the economic agenda. At every negotiation with the EU the City's interests are paramount. The notorious 'five conditions' for UK entry into the Single Currency which some bright spark at the Treasury persuaded Gordon Brown to adopt early in his term as Chancellor, refer in *general* terms to the effect of Single Currency membership on the rest of the economy, but *specifically* includes Single Currency membership's effect on the City.

The City has had complete control of the UK's economic policies since 1979. The last flicker of resistance by Labour to the City's agenda occurred about a year before the election of 1997 when, for a few weeks, Will Hutton's take on the City-versus-industry thesis, his idea of the Stakeholder Economy, was apparently being taken seriously by Tony Blair, until the idea was run past Labour's contacts in the City.

> 'One minute the then-editor of *The Observer* [Will Hutton] was sitting in Blair's kitchen, watching Tony push down the plunger on the cafetiere, as he said, "Will, stakeholding is going to be our *Bible*." (The notion had been at the core of *The State We're In*, Hutton's runaway best-seller which persuaded large numbers of people to join Blair's rebranded New Labour.) Just six weeks later Hutton found his idea had been

dropped, after Blair's adoption of it had been greeted with suspicion in the business world...'[9]

This account was confirmed by the Australian academic Shann Turnbull, who has proposed a slightly different version of the stakeholder concept. Turnbull wrote:

'When I met Geoff Mulgan [one of New Labour's policy advisors in No.10 Downing Street] back in Australia on his honeymoon in 1998 he advised me that stakeholder idea had frightened *the big end of town* and so it had been dropped. Company directors were concerned that they would be made accountable to people other than shareholders and institutional investors were frightened that it would destroy shareholder value.'[10] (Emphasis added.)

'The big end of town' being the City of London is an interesting image. But how big is it? How important is the City to the UK economy? What proportion of the Gross Domestic Product is the City? To have this much power it must be big. At least as big, say, as manufacturing, which has been persistently cut down in the City's interests for the past 20 years. *Wrong*. According to figures produced in 1999 by the City of London's own propaganda outfit, British Invisibles (which may be presumed to exaggerate somewhat in the City's favour) the City contributed 6.4% of the UK GDP. That is not a misprint: 6.4%. Manufacturing, by contrast, is still, even after twenty years of assault, somewhere between 20% and 30%, depending on how you define manufacturing.[11] And, let it be noted, that 6.4% is now mostly owned by Americans. The reorganisation of the City, the so-called 'big bang' in 1986, was the beginning of the end for British ownership of the City. These days it is essentially a branch office of Wall Street.[12]

Pursuing 'the knowledge economy' (Blair) and 'an enterprise culture open to all' (Brown), Blair and Brown may now believe they are on the wave of the future, driven by technology and changing world markets; but the truth is that at the end of the 1980s they simply swallowed whole the ideology of the City of London (the pioneers of globalisation, after all) and adopted its policies, which reflect its interests. The result has been, just as it was under Mrs Thatcher, who was pursuing the same policies, the continued destruction of the manufacturing base of the UK.

A Disinformation Operation

'I have taken from my party everything they thought they believed in. What keeps it together is success and power.'

- attributed to Tony Blair by Andrew Rawnsley
in his *Servants Of The People*
(2001 paperback edition), page 195.

The capture of the Labour Party by the Blair/Brown faction has been the most successful political disinformation operation I know of in the UK's political history. Those to be disinformed were: the unions, who used to fund most of it but whose share of Labour's funding is now down to around 50%; the party's members, who funded part of it and did the work; and MPs. The union officials eventually realised what the game was but had nowhere else to go. Only one union had withdrawn some of its political funding by the election of 2001. The members of the party were too ill-informed to grasp what was going on, unable to find a means of opposing it or incapable of believing that the New Labour faction really meant what they said. Many party members trust their leaders and they were placated by periodic statements proclaiming that Labour *values* were still in place, while Labour *policies* were removed or undermined. They were also reassured by the presence of the totemic figure of John Prescott at the elbow of the Brown/Blair group. The MPs were generally bought off with the prospect of election victory or 'disciplined' by the fear of another loss (however unlikely that seemed after 1994) for which they might be blamed.

In 1997 I gave a talk to my own branch of the Labour Party and laid out a simplified version of the thesis in this book before them. Nobody took it seriously. I didn't expect them to. I had already tried, and largely failed, to persuade the members of my branch of the Labour Party that the Militant Tendency really was the conspiracy in the party that the party's leaders, various Militant defectors and a couple of well-researched books said it was. People who attend meetings of political parties, the dreaded 'activists,' may be a tiny self-selecting minority but they seem to be no more able to confront difficult problems than any other group. I was in Hartlepool on the night of the election of 2001 and watched the Hartlepool Labour Party members cheer as Peter Mandelson entered the sports centre in which the vote count was taking place. Labour's policies? They just looked thrilled to have a celebrity as their MP.

It is all deeply depressing at one level, and hilarious at another. Based on nothing more than a hunch about the shape of the future, a *Labour* Government is pissing away what was left of the manufacturing base after the Thatcher Governments had a go at it. The UK's fishing industry was largely wrecked as part of the price of entering the EEC in 1972. The steel industry was 'rationalised' and, like coal, was mostly closed in the 1980s. Agriculture is being reduced under 'set aside' schemes, another chunk will vanish as a result of the foot and mouth outbreak, and a further section will go as the result of the collapse of farming incomes in the last three years caused by the low payments made in 'green pounds' (i.e. Euros) via UK membership of the EU's Common Agricultural Policy. But never mind, eh? Trust your Uncle Tony. He may not know how to use a PC but he knows we have 'the knowledge economy' coming over the horizon and everything is going to be OK.

And perhaps it will. Perhaps we will all end up in 'the knowledge economy' (whatever that is) and we won't need fishing, farming, steel-making, mining, machine tools and manufacturing in the future. What am I complaining about? Labour's policies are working. Unemployment fell in the same month that manufacturing officially went into recession. Perhaps the neo-liberals are right. Perhaps the service sector *can* replace manufacturing.

But it can't. The service sector has *not* replaced the manufacturing destroyed by its policies in the last 20 years. Britain is running a huge, and growing, trade deficit which is not permanently sustainable. Thus far only a bunch of the 'old lags,' the unreconstructed Keynesians, as Gordon Brown probably thinks of them, are worried by this.[13] I'm with them. I cling to the now old-fashioned idea that on a small island with a population of 60 million it is madness to let the island's productive resources be abandoned. I think Labour's leaders have got it completely wrong and however they think of themselves, history will judge that the Blair/Brown faction was merely the ultimate triumph of the ideology of the City over the rest of us. And, let us hope, the last dribble of Thatcherism down the leg of British politics.

Notes

1. For any reader still uncertain about how this works... Interest rates higher than those of other countries push up the value of the currency. Increases in the value of the currency make imports cheaper and exports more expensive. So the relative level of interest rates is critical.

2. Nigel Lawson was trying to get this done in 1988 but Prime Minister Thatcher blocked it. See Nigel Lawson, *The View From No.11* (London: Corgi, 1992), pages 869/70. The financial press, reflecting the views and interests of the City, could see higher interest rates coming and were thrilled by Brown's decision. See Paul Routledge, *Gordon Brown: The Biography* (London: Simon and Schuster, 1998), page 294.

3. As I typed this sentence I found myself wondering for the umpteenth time: can he really be this naive? The answer still looks like 'yes' to me. There is no rabbit waiting to be pulled from the hat.

4. Probably the latter. The parallels with the Thatcher/Howe regime arise again. Like them, Brown seems to have believed that if domestic inflation is low everything else slots into place, automatically.

5. See for example: David Smith et al, 'Strong Pound Drives Up Insolvencies,' *The Sunday Times* (*Business*), 22 February 1998; Charlotte Denning, 'Trade Slumps Into The Red,' *The Guardian*, 24 June 1998; Larry Elliot, 'Circular Walk Along The Third Way,' *The Guardian*, 6 July 1998; Peter Kellner, 'How The Bank Has Been Taking Us All For A Ride,' *Evening Standard*, 4 August 1998; Mark Atkinson, 'Brown Attacked By Benn,' *The Guardian*, 14 August 1998; Bill Jamieson, 'EEF Slams "Arrogant" Treasury,' *The Sunday Telegraph*, 13 September 1998; Larry Elliot, 'Brown Proves A Covert Radical,' *The Guardian*, 21 December 1998. 'His reluctance to even attempt to talk down the level of Sterling seems bizarre, given what the confederation of British Industry has been saying about exporters' prospects.'; Larry Elliot, 'Sweet Talk Won't Stop Sterling Now,' *The Guardian*, 10 May 1999. 'On the one hand a Government which has its roots in Britain's manufacturing heartlands and professes to want to join the single currency; on the other an exchange rate that will close factories and preclude membership of the single currency.'; Charlotte Denny, 'London Visitors Fail To Impress Metal Bashers,' *The Guardian*, 20 May 1999, which quoted a Midlands 'metal basher' that they had had the Governor of the Bank of England in Birmingham the night before 'who went on record as saying he was not prepared to offer any solace to manufacturing whatsoever.'; William Keegan, 'Gordon's "Stability" Is Anything But,' *The Observer*, 23 May 1999, quoted testimony from James Dyson before a Lords committee that 'the double whammy' of a strong pound and interest rates at twice the European level 'were a very high price to pay' for the Chancellor's 'stable environment... there may not be any industry left.'; Philip Thornton, 'North To Suffer Recession This Year,' *The Independent*, 4 August 1999, quoting Adam

Cole, economist with HSBC. 'The current mix of growth looks worryingly similar to the 1980s.'

6. *The Guardian*, 11 June 1999.

7. The oddity is that Brown appears to believe that something new is going on. He seems to have forgotten that in the 1950s and 1960s the policy of putting up interest rates and clobbering the domestic economy as soon as a little inflation appeared was derided by Labour spokespeople as 'stop-go' economics.

8. Will Hutton, *The Observer*, 2 May 1999.

9. Paul Vallely, 'Enemies Of The People,' *The Independent* (*Review*), 4 July 2000.

10. This was in an e-mail posted on the Net as 'OWNERSHIP: Re: HOMESTEAD: No 3rd Way?' from Shann Turnbull (sturnbull@mba1963.hbs.edu) on 25 May 2000. Turnbull's Website is http:// members.optusnet.com.au/~sturnbull/index.html

A significant part of New Labour's relations with the City involves Gavyn Davies, Chief Economist at the American bank Goldman Sachs. His wife has been Gordon Brown's PA for many years. In a profile of Davies by Brian Milton written for, but not published by, *London Financial News* of 10 June 1996, Milton quoted a 'Labour source' as saying: 'Gavyn doesn't write policy, but he is our own City sounding board. We draft the ideas and Gavyn tells us what the effect will be on the economy and what the response will be in the markets.' No wonder Goldman Sachs made him a partner, now worth about £50 (or is it £100?) million! The Milton article got as far as page make-up before being rejected. I was sent a copy of the page.

11. See Oliver Morgan, 'Official Figures Hide Manufacturing Jobs,' *The Observer* (*Business*), 22 October 2000, which suggests that more careful analysis of the categories gives manufacturing something like 28% of the British GDP.

Why manufacturing in the UK has so little political influence is one of the central issues of our post-war history.

12. The impact of the 'big bang' is clearly described in Philip Augar, *The Death Of Gentlemanly Capitalism* (Harmondsworth: Penguin, 2000).

13. See for example Ian Aitken, 'This Country's Living Beyond Its Means,' *The Guardian*, 28 May 2001.

The Essential Library: Currently Available

Film Directors:

Woody Allen (Revised)	Tim Burton	Ang Lee
Jane Campion (£2.99)	John Carpenter	Steve Soderbergh
Jackie Chan	Joel & Ethan Coen	Clint Eastwood
David Cronenberg	Terry Gilliam (£2.99)	
Alfred Hitchcock	Krzysztof Kieslowski (£2.99)	
Stanley Kubrick	Sergio Leone	
David Lynch	Brian De Palma (£2.99)	
Sam Peckinpah (£2.99)	Ridley Scott	
Orson Welles	Billy Wilder	
Steven Spielberg	Mike Hodges	

Film Genres:

Film Noir	Hong Kong Heroic Bloodshed (£2.99)
Horror Films	Slasher Movies
Spaghetti Westerns	Vampire Films (£2.99)
Blaxploitation Films	Bollywood
French New Wave	

Film Subjects:

Laurel & Hardy	Marx Brothers
Steve McQueen (£2.99)	Marilyn Monroe
The Oscars®	Filming On A Microbudget
Bruce Lee	Film Music

TV:

Doctor Who

Literature:

Cyberpunk	Philip K Dick
Agatha Christie	Noir Fiction (£2.99)
Terry Pratchett	Sherlock Holmes
Hitchhiker's Guide	Alan Moore

Ideas:

Conspiracy Theories	Nietzsche
Feminism	Freud & Psychoanalysis

History:

Alchemy & Alchemists	The Crusades
American Civl War	American Indian Wars
The Black Death	Jack The Ripper
The Rise Of New Labour	Ancient Greece

Available at all good bookstores or send a cheque (payable to 'Oldcastle Books') to: **Pocket Essentials (Dept RNL), 18 Coleswood Rd, Harpenden, Herts, AL5 1EQ, UK.** £3.99 each unless otherwise stated. For each book add 50p postage & packing in the UK and £1 elsewhere.